Mufti,

Eleme...
puter g...

D0765683

DATE DUE

ELEMENTARY COMPUTER GRAPHICS

ELEMENTARY COMPUTER GRAPHICS

Aftab A. Mufti

Professor of Computer Science and Engineering
Technical University of Nova Scotia
Halifax, Nova Scotia

RESTON PUBLISHING COMPANY, INC.

A Prentice-Hall Company

RESTON, VIRGINIA 22090

Library of Congress Cataloging in Publication Data

Mufti, Aftab A.
    Elementary computer graphics.

    Includes bibliographies.
    1. Computer graphics.   I. Title.
T385.M83   1982   001.64'43   82-20468
ISBN 0-8359-1654-5

10   9   8   7   6   5   4   3   2   1

Interior design and production: Jack Zibulsky

This book is dedicated to my son
JAVED CHRISTOPHER MUFTI

CONTENTS

PREFACE

This book is addressed to those who are exploring computer graphics for the first time. As an introductory book on the subject, ELEMENTARY COMPUTER GRAPHICS is useful to both engineers and computer scientists. The overview of computer graphics and the fundamental ideas of mathematics, data structures and color useful in computer graphics are explained in Chapters 1 through 5. Two-dimensional and three-dimensional graphics are covered in Chapters 6 and 7 respectively. Chapter 8 gives an application of computer graphics systems to engineering science problems. Chapter 9 briefly describes computer graphics methods using a microcomputer. FORTRAN is used as a computer language for programming the text with the exception of Chapter 9 throughout.

ACKNOWLEDGEMENTS

The author gratefully acknowledges the encouragement and support of Professors Leslie G. Jaeger and Whitman Wright. Professor Jaeger read the manuscript and made valuable suggestions. Professor Wright provided material for the chapter on hardware. I am indebted to both of them as friends and colleagues.

The author would also like to acknowledge the assistance of many individuals at the Technical University of Nova Scotia—specifically Amrish Choxi who assisted in checking the programs, proofing the manuscript and preparing the illustrations.

Thanks to Mrs. Ann Doiron who handled the typing of the manuscript and related functions of composition. Her excellent performance has significantly shortened the time from the concept of the text to its publication.

Finally, I want to express my thanks to the editors and reviewers whose helpful advice and suggestions made the text more valuable.

1
OVERVIEW
OF
COMPUTER
GRAPHICS

1.1 INTRODUCTION

In several branches of engineering and architecture, the designer/analyst is faced with the problem of imagining geometric objects in two-dimensional and three-dimensional spaces. Once the imagination is translated into a design, illustrations have to be drawn to achieve the material construction of these objects. Therefore, we have to develop the knowledge that will translate a thousand words into one picture. In computing, it is certainly true that one picture can be considerably more valuable than several yards of line printer output. This is all the more true if an engineer has to interpret the output and take further action on it with the computer.

The recent development of computer graphics devices opens up a completely new range of fields of application for computers. For the first time, an engineer can have direct access to the power of a computer, communicating in visual terms which are natural to man. As the complexity of the engineering system under a computer study increases, the time spent by an engineer and the likelihood of committing errors increases at a very high rate; thus, it becomes very important for him to use a computer with a graphic system. This will open new vistas and present the engineer with opportunities to make full use of design skills in order to build a world in which mankind is freed from the drudgery that has haunted its past.

There are several engineering and scientific applications of computer graphics. The well-known ones are:

1. Computer-aided design
2. Computer-aided manufacturing
3. Computer-aided drafting
4. Real-time process control
5. Manipulation of cartographic data
6. Real-time simulation and training
7. Automobile, aircraft, and ship design
8. Integrated circuit layout
9. Architecture and structural design
10. Air-control systems

1.2 BASIC DEFINITIONS

It is essential to discuss the terminology associated with the subject of computer graphics in order to introduce a reader to the subject. Since the inception of computer graphics in the 1960s, the field has captured the imagination and technical interest of a rapidly increasing number of individuals from many disciplines. The field of computer graphics is expanding rapidly and it combines the age-old art of graphical communication and the new technology of computers.

A number of terms and definitions are used rather loosely in this field:

1. Computer-Aided Design (CAD)
2. Computer-Aided Design and Drafting (CADD)
3. Computer-Aided Manufacturing (CAM)
4. Computer Graphics (CG)
5. Interactive Graphics (IG)

These are used interchangably or in such a manner that considerable confusion exists as to their precise meaning. Therefore, these terms should be defined and differentiated as much as possible.

Of these terms, CAD is the most general. CAD may be defined as any use of the computer to aid in the design of the individual part, a subsystem, or a total system. The use does not have to involve graphics. The design process may be at the system concept level or at the detailed part-design level. It may also involve an interface with CAM. However, when drafting is included as a part of computer-aided design, computer graphics is an essential component of CADD.

Computer-aided manufacturing is the use of a computer to aid in the manufacture or production of a part, exclusive of the design process. A direct interface between the results of a CAD application and the necessary part programming using such language as APT (Automatic Programmed Tools) and UNIAPT (United's APT), the direction of a machine tool using a hardwired or softwired (minicomputer) controller to read data from a punched paper tape and generate the necessary commands to control a machine tool, or the direct control of a machine tool using a minicomputer may be involved.

Computer graphics is the use of a computer to define, store, manipulate, interrogate, and present pictorial output. This is essentially a passive operation. The computer prepares and presents stored information to an observer in the form of pictures. The observer has no direct control over the picture that is being presented. The application may be as simple as the presentation of the graph of a single function using a high-speed line printer or a time-sharing teletype terminal, or as complex as the simulation of the automatic re-entry and landing of a space capsule.

Interactive graphics also uses the computer to prepare and present pictorial material. However, in interactive graphics the observer can influence the picture as it is being presented—i.e., the observer interacts with the picture in real time. To see the importance of the real-time restriction, consider the problem of rotating a complex three-dimensional picture composed of 1000 lines at a reasonable rotation rate—say, 15°/s. As we shall see subsequently, the 1000 lines of the picture are most conveniently represented by a 1000×4 matrix of homogeneous coordinates of the end points of the lines, and the rotation is most conveniently accomplished by multiplying this 1000×4 matrix by a 4×4 transformation matrix. Accomplishing the required matrix multiplication requires 16,000 multiplications, 12,000 additions, and 1000 divisions. If this matrix multiplication is accomplished in software, the time is significant. To see this, consider that a typical minicomputer using a hardware floating-point processor requires 6 microseconds to multiply two numbers, 4 microseconds to add two numbers, and 8 microseconds to divide two numbers. Thus, the matrix multiplication requires 0.15 seconds.

Since computer displays that allow dynamic motion require that the picture be redrawn (refreshed) at least 30 times each second in order to avoid flicker, it is obvious that the picture cannot change smoothly. Even if it is assumed that the picture is recalculated (updated) only 15 times each second—i.e., every degree—it is still not possible to accomplish a smooth rotation in software. Thus, this is now no longer interactive graphics. To regain the ability to present the picture interactively, several things can be done: (a) Clever programming can reduce the time to accomplish the required matrix multiplication; however, a point will be reached at which this is no longer possible. (b) The complexity of the picture can be reduced; in this case, the resulting picture may not be acceptable. (c) Finally, the matrix multiplication can be accomplished by using a special-purpose digital hardware matrix multiplier; this is the most promising approach—it can easily handle the problem outlined above.

1.3 HISTORY OF COMPUTER GRAPHICS

In 1950, the first computer-driven display attached to MIT's Whirlwind I computer was used to generate simple pictures. This display made use of a cathode-ray tube (CRT) similar to one used in television sets. Several years earlier, a CRT had been used as an information storage device; this technique was to emerge years later, in the form of a storage CRT incorporated in many low-cost interactive graphic terminals.

During the 1950s, interactive computer graphics made little progress because the computers of that period were not suited to interactive use. These computers were "number crunchers" that performed lengthy calculations for physicists and missile designers. Only toward the end of the decade, with the development of machines like MIT's TX-0 and TX-2, did interactive computing become feasible, and interest in computer graphics then began to increase rapidly.

The single event that did most to promote interactive computer graphics as an important new field was the publication in 1962 of a brilliant thesis by Ivan E. Sutherland, who had just received his Ph.D. from MIT. This thesis, entitled "Sketchpad: A Man-Machine Graphical Communication System," proved to many readers that interactive computer graphics was a viable, useful, and exciting field of research. By the mid 1960s, large computer graphics research projects were started at MIT, General Motors, Bell Telephone laboratories, and Lockheed Aircraft; the glorious age of computer graphics has begun.

If the 1960s represent the heady years of computer graphics research, the 1970s have been the decade in which this research began to bear fruit.

Interactive graphics displays are now in use in many countries and are widely used for educational purposes, even in elementary schools. The instant appeal of computer graphics to users of all ages has helped it to spread into many applications and will undoubtedly guarantee its continued growth in popularity.

1.4 PROPERTIES OF THE HUMAN VISUAL SYSTEM

Another important subject which should be studied in relation to computer graphics is the human visual system.
Some relevant aspects are:

1. Brightness discrimination
2. Flicker
3. Fusion
4. Visual resolution
5. Energy detection

1.4.1 Brightness Discrimination

The amount of light that must be added to a uniformly illuminated field in order to be noticeable is proportional to the total illumination of the field. For example, on a sunny day at the beach it is impossible to detect the light of a candle on the sand, but on a moonless night, it will appear quite bright.

1.4.2 Flicker

When a light is turned on and off rapidly, it appears to flicker. As the rate at which the light is turned on and off increases, it appears to flicker more and more rapidly. At some frequency, the flicker is no longer perceived and the light appears to be steady. This frequency is called the fusion point, and it is about 48 flickers/s for the human eye. (See, however, the comment in Sec. 1.4.3 below.)

1.4.3 Fusion

The fusion point is also a function of the level of illumination. The higher the level of illumination, the higher the frequency at which fusion occurs. We note that fusion can occur at a frequency as low as a few cycles/s at very low levels of illumination. This is very important in the design of display systems.

1.4.4 Visual Resolution

The eye contains two types of receptors: rods and cones. The cones are distributed with highest density in the center of the eye, with the rods off-center (see Fig. 1.1).

1.4.5 Energy Detection

The eye is an extremely efficient detector of radiant energy. In a dark-adapted eye, a few photons can lead to perception of light. The rods are more sensitive light energy detectors than the cones. The cones have high spatial resolution (acuity). The higher the brightness level (within reason), the greater the visual acuity.

1.4.6 Visual Fatigue

Prolonged exposure to high brightness leads to visual fatigue. Glare is a particularly serious cause of visual fatigue. By keeping the brightness level to a workable minimum and avoiding glare, visual fatigue will be minimized. This also lowers the fusion point and reduces visual acuity.

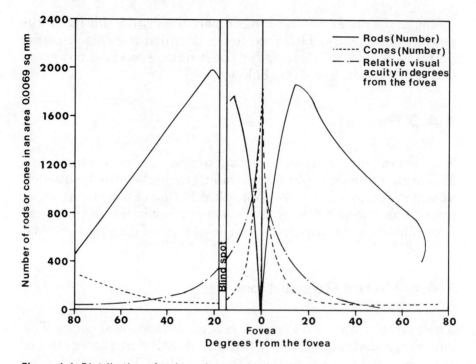

Figure 1.1 Distribution of rods and cones in the eye

1.5 COLOR FUNDAMENTALS

Color forms one of the most intimate contacts in our every-day life. We wear colored clothes, we use colored objects, we live in colored houses, and we eat colored food. However, color is a perceptual, not physical, phenomenon. In general, the eye responds to long, middle, and short wavelengths which correspond to the sensations red, green, and blue. The light consists of a continuous spectrum of colors, ranging from violet at one end to red at the other (see Fig. 1.2).

The spectrum may be broadly divided into six regions: violet, blue, green, yellow, orange, and red. From the scale that appears in Fig. 1.3, it is seen that no color ends abruptly

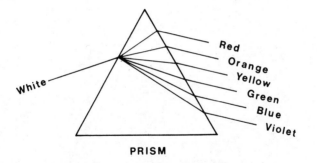

Figure 1.2 Various colors of white light

at a specific point, but rather that each color gradually blends into the next.

The reason three primaries were chosen, in preference to four, stems from the theory that the eye behaves as though it contains three sets of nerves with each set of nerves responsive to a different portion of the visible spectrum. Thus, one set of nerves has its greatest sensitivity in the blue region, another set is most sensitive in the green region, and the third set is most sensitive to red.

For many years, it was believed that the ability of the human eye to see color was the same whether the area viewed was large or small. This has been found to be untrue. Therefore, color can be presented in broader "patches" and need not be as finely detailed as geometry.

1.6 COLOR MIXTURES

We can form different colors by adding varying intensities of red, green, and blue primary colors.

Ultra Violet	Violet	Blue	Green	Yellow	Orange	Red	Infrared
	400	450	500	570	590	610	700

Millimicrons

Figure 1.3 The broad color regions of the visible spectrum

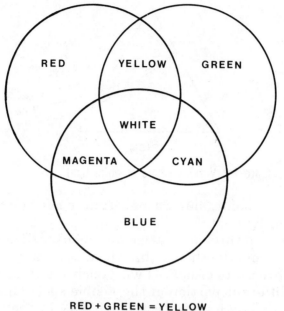

RED + GREEN = YELLOW
RED + BLUE = MAGENTA
BLUE + GREEN = CYAN
RED + GREEN + BLUE = WHITE

Figure 1.4 Additive color

The rules shown in Fig. 1.4 apply for additive color combination. Thus, for example, yellow can be formed by combining red and green. White can be produced by combining red, green, and blue.

We can also form different colors by subtracting various intensities of red, green, and blue primary colors. For subtraction, we have to use filters, as shown in Fig. 1.5. Each filter absorbs one of the primaries. For example, yellow absorbs blue and allows red and green. Thus, we can use complementary filters to produce primaries.

In Fig. 1.6, a diagram is shown that indicates the colors produced by either adding or subtracting the primary colors.

In Fig. 1.7, it is shown that when drawing colored lines on a screen, or a film, two primaries will produce a complementary color. To avoid this condition, two lines are drawn by using a primary color for one line and a complementary color

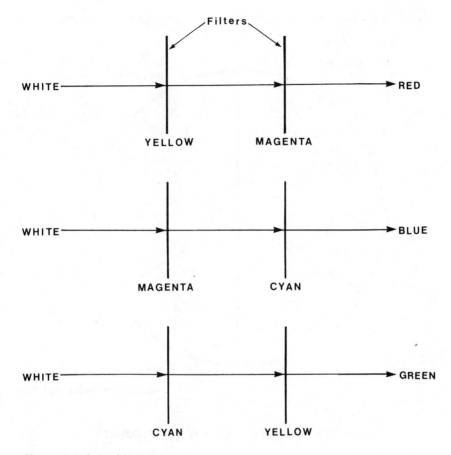

Figure 1.5 Color filters

(not the complement of the primary) for the other line (see Fig. 1.8).

1.7 HUMAN VISION AND COMPUTER GRAPHICS

Why should computer graphics concern itself with human vision? This question is extremely important from the standpoint of the design of graphics terminals and display techniques. The graphic output devices shift the burden of inte-

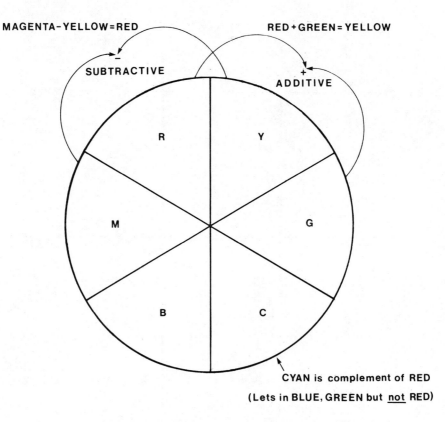

COLORS ON OPPOSITE SIDES ARE COMPLEMENTS

Figure 1.6 Adding versus subtracting colors

grating information generated by computers onto the human vision system. The human vision system consists of hundreds of successive two-dimensional arrays of millions of interconnected parallel computers. Perception seems instantaneous because we are not conscious of the massive amounts of computation that occur. What we consciously see at a glance is already a highly structured, synthesized, and summarized version of the actual light intensity mosaic that is perceived by the human brain.

We need to know what characteristics of visual presenta-

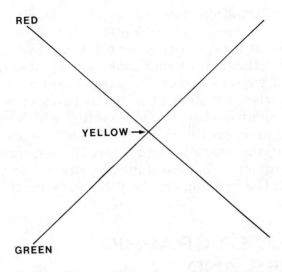

Figure 1.7 Intersection of two primary colors

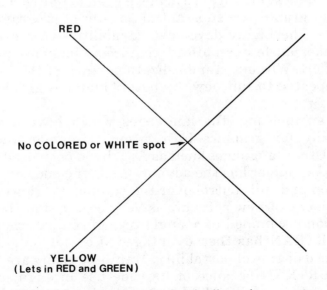

Figure 1.8 Intersection of red and yellow color

tion make information stand out quickly, clearly, without distortion, and without conscious effort. We should be able to eliminate, or at least compensate for, kinks in a graphic output, flicker of the picture, and poor coloring of scenes. Therefore, we must characterize the parameters which influence the human visual system and should be incorporated carefully in a display device. The parameters which characterize the display and specify its performance include the flicker rate, resolution, intensity, and color. The optimum selection of these parameters is determined by the purpose of the display, within the limiting constraints of complexity and cost.

1.8 COMPUTER GRAPHIC LANGUAGES AND STANDARDS

The slow development of standards and suitable programming languages has delayed the development and use of computer graphics software. To achieve even a limited amount in computer graphics, a substantial amount of programming is required. The highly developed capabilities that everybody would like, but few can afford, require an immense programming effort. Without standardization, much of this work has to be repeated to suit new computers and new graphic hardware.

In engineering, the languages which have been used principally for graphics have been Assembler and FORTRAN. Other languages such as APL have been used to some extent. Assembler has the advantage of efficiency of program execution and full control over the equipment. However, the development of new software is very costly, and the implementation is confined to a single type of computer.

FORTRAN has the advantages of easier programming and a good degree of portability. Many engineers are familiar with FORTRAN because of its wide use in engineering. A useful feature of FORTRAN for graphics is its ability to make use of subroutines written in Assembler. This permits the full power of the particular computer to be utilized when some special task such as hidden line removal has to be undertaken, and when the economic benefits justify the necessary programming effort.

ANSI 66 FORTRAN (the only standard FORTRAN still available on some equipment) has some limitations for graphic use, as follows:

1. The most immediate and obvious limitation is that FORTRAN, by itself, does not give the programmer the capability of writing a program that will generate the bit strings necessary to drive the graphic equipment. A limited amount of Assembler programming is required to do this. A very good practice is to confine the Assembler programming to the smallest possible amount, and to define a clear interface between the FORTRAN and the Assembler portions of the work.

2. ANSI 66 FORTRAN utilizes only sequential files, thereby making it very difficult to develop an efficient graphics data base in a standard manner. Although not important for some applications, this lack of an adequate file-handling capability is very important for others.

3. ANSI 66 FORTRAN does not have facilities for file management at run time. This is important in many graphic applications.

4. ANSI 66 FORTRAN lacks the facilities to write structured programs, hence slowing the writing of graphic software and making its maintenance more difficult.

ANSI 77 FORTRAN, now a CSA and ANSI standard, overcomes or at least relieves most (but not all) of the difficulties just cited. It provides for character variables, thus clearing up a persistent problem with ANSI 66 FORTRAN with some bearing on graphics; it provides for direct access files; it has some useful file-management facilities; and it has limited but probably adequate provisions for structured programming. The author is not aware of any attempt to apply ANSI 77 FORTRAN in a serious way to computer graphics. However, such a development should be expected before too long.

The next generation of FORTRAN (now called FORTRAN 8X), which is still under development, will be different in structure from present-day FORTRAN in that it will be possible to extend the compiler in a modular manner to support specialized areas such as graphics.

The languages APL and BASIC are attractive to the graphic programmer because of the relative ease of programming. However, for complex and large volume work, the resulting programs are slow in execution unless they can be "compiled" rather than run in an interpretive mode. At present, the programming languages BASIC and another new favorite, PASCAL, suffer from lack of standardization at a sufficiently high level to be really useful.

The language GRAPPLE, developed by Bell Northern Research in Ottawa, Canada, provides well-developed two-dimensional graphic capabilities at the language level and has much to offer the graphic programmer. It permits him or her to start programming at the application level with a standard set of graphic capabilities already in place. However, the language is not widely used at present. In the past, it has to be re-implemented laboriously on each new computer, a difficulty which is just now being overcome.

A lack of industry-wide standards has caused problems not only at the software level but at the equipment level. Different plotters require different sets of primitive commands to drive them, and when they have intelligence it is organized according to the equipment.

The lack of standards in computer graphics software and hardware has brought some response from the user community. In the early 1970s, Applied Research Ltd., in Cambridge, England, produced a set of graphic standards called GINO. These standards have been extended and are in use today in some British software. In the United States, SIG-GRAPH, a committee of the American Computer Machinery Society (ACM), has been instrumental in developing guidelines which it is expected will become the basis for future standards. The Programming Languages Committee of the Canadian Standards Association has recently formed a working group on computer graphics.

Up to now, the work on computer graphic standards has proceeded very slowly. One of the problems appears to be that many people are looking for a single set of graphic standards. Yet the field of computer graphics is so broad and the applications so diversified that agreement by all the interested parties is next to impossible. If anything at all is to be achieved, some of this attempt at generality and universality may have to be abandoned. This is in fact what has happened with the programming languages such as FORTRAN, PL/1, and PASCAL, which are now in competition for survival.

SUMMARY

In this chapter, basic definitions and concepts used in computer graphics, such as passive graphics, interactive graphics, and computer-aided design and manufacturing are described. The characteristics of vision, color, and their effect on the graphical display monitor are discussed.

Finally, a justification is given with respect to the choice of FORTRAN language for writing computer graphics programs for this text.

REFERENCES

Chasen, S. H., *Geometric Principles and Procedures for Computer Graphic Applications* (Englewood Cliffs, New Jersey: Prentice-Hall, 1978).

Cornsweet, T. N., *Visual Perception* (New York: Academic Press, 1970).

Foley, J. D. and Van Dam, A., *Fundamentals of Interactive Computer Graphics* (Reading, Massachusetts: Addison-Wesley, 1982).

Gilio, W. K., *Interactive Computer Graphics* (Englewood Cliffs, New Jersey: Prentice-Hall, 1978).

Kiver, S. K., *Color Television Fundamentals* (New York: McGraw-Hill Book Company, 1964).

Mitchell, W. J., *Computer Aided Architectural Design* (New York: Petrocelli Charter, 1977).

Mufti, A. A. and Jaeger, L. G., "FORTRAN—Should This Be an Engineers' Computer Language?", Canadian Society for Civil Engineers Annual Conference, University of New Brunswick, Fredericton, Canada, May 1981.

Newmann, W. M. and Sproull, R. F., *Principles of Interactive Computer Graphics* (New York: McGraw-Hill Book Company, 1979).

Parslow, R. D., Prowse, R. W., and Green, R. W., *Computer Graphics* (New York: Plenum Press, 1969).

Rogers, D. F. and Adams, J. A., *Mathematical Elements for Computer Graphics* (New York: McGraw-Hill Book Company, 1976).

Sutherland, I. E., "Sketchpad: A Man-Machine Graphic Communication System," AFIPS Conference Proceedings, Spring Joint Computer Conference, Baltimore, Maryland, 1963.

2
COMPUTER
GRAPHICS
HARDWARE

2.1 INTRODUCTION

To a person unfamiliar with computer graphics, there appears to be a bewildering variety of hardware commercially available. One's choice of hardware will depend largely upon the type of computer graphics activity that will be undertaken.

2.2 GRAPHIC DATA DISPLAY EQUIPMENT

It is useful to make a distinction between graphic display equipment and graphic data input equipment, even though certain equipment can be made to serve both purposes.

With graphic display hardware, the major distinction is between devices such as plotters that produce a relatively permanent form of output, for instance, drawings on paper or Mylar, and cathode-ray tube terminals (CRTs) that provide a quick and convenient but temporary display.

2.2.1 Plotters

There are a variety of options available for plotters, which will be discussed below. There are two major ways of displaying the graphic information, as follows:

1. By means of a series of lines or vectors, drawn line by line, known as vector displays, illustrated in Fig. 2.1(a), (b). A small and a larger vector plotter are shown in Figs. 2.2 and 2.3.

2. By means of a two-dimensional array of black or colored point dots known as a "matrix display," somewhat like the method used to represent pictures in a newspaper, illustrated in Fig. 2.1(c).

Color can be obtained, easily in the case of multiple pen vector plotters, and with somewhat more expense, with some matrix plotters.

2.2.2 Cathode-Ray Tube Terminals

As with the plotters, there is an important distinction between the vector cathode-ray tubes which draw line by line and the matrix-type cathode-ray tubes which display their graphic information dot by dot. Partly because of their affinity to the type of display that occurs on a television screen, matrix-type plots on the screen of a CRT graphics terminal are called *raster displays*.

With vector-type cathode-ray tube terminals, a further important distinction is between the "refresh" tubes which are capable of displaying motion, and the "storage" tubes which cannot display motion although they have other attractive features.

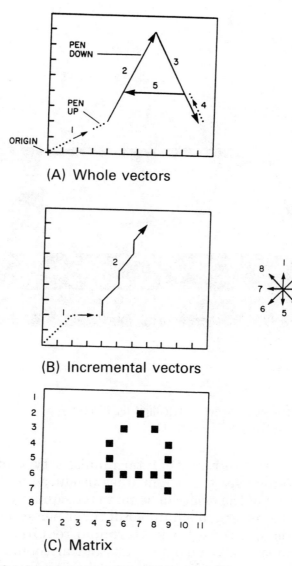

(A) Whole vectors

(B) Incremental vectors

(C) Matrix

Figure 2.1 Representation of a graphic object using
different types of displays

Figure 2.2 A small vector plotter digitizer (Courtesy of Tektronix Canada, Ltd.)

With the refresh CRT terminals, a type of phosphor is used that causes the bright lines produced on the screen by the impact of the electron beam to fade quickly, requiring the tube to be refreshed a number of times per second. This characteristic of a refresh CRT terminal requires a complex refresh controller, consumes substantial computing power if the total amount of linework displayed on the screen is large, and can cause image instability and flickering. However, it also enables the image on the screen to undergo rapid modification, permitting selective erasure or depiction of motion.

The graphic storage CRT terminal stores the image on the screen without the need for refreshing. The advantages of the storage CRT terminal include a high degree of image

Figure 2.3 A medium-size drum-type vector plotter

precision and stability, and the ability to display complex images while utilizing very little computing power. Disadvantages are its inability to perform selective erasure or to show motion. In the recent past, storage CRT terminals such as the Tektronix 4014 (Figs. 2.4 and 2.5) have become considerably less expensive than refresh CRT terminals with comparable image quality and static display power. Hence, they have been very popular for many engineering applications. However, still more recently, certain raster display CRT terminals have become much less expensive and are now offering stiff competition.

Some recently developed CRT terminals combine a storage and a refresh capability. The portion of the image that is refreshed is displayed with less intensity than the portion which remains static. The refresh portion can show motion, undergo selective erasure, and display a substantial amount of linework.

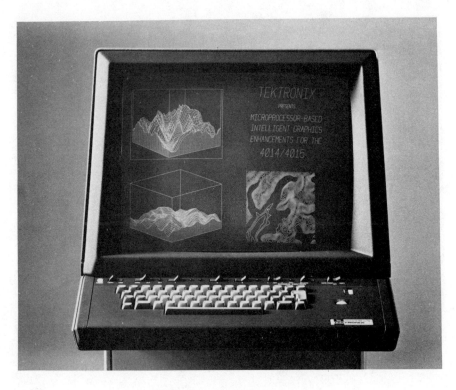

Figure 2.4 A Tektronix 4014 storage cathode-ray tube terminal (Courtesy of Tektronic Canada, Ltd.)

2.3 LOCAL INTELLIGENCE OF DISPLAY EQUIPMENT

Some of the graphic display equipment has substantial local intelligence and can respond to general instructions to draw simple curves, dashed lines, and scaled and rotated text, and even perform relatively complex graphics tasks. Other equipment is almost devoid of intelligence and must be directed in full detail to draw point after point or line after line. The question of display unit intelligence will be dealt with in more

Figure 2.5 A Tektronix 4014 CRT terminal with an interactive graphics menu on the right-hand
side of the screen (Courtesy of Tektronix
Canada, Ltd.)

detail later. A summary of some of the possibilities is given in
Fig. 2.6.

2.4 GRAPHIC DATA
INPUT EQUIPMENT

With graphics data input equipment, an important distinction is between the digitizing table (or tablet) and the CRT
terminal, here functioning as an input device. Both types of

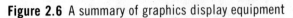

PLOTTERS	{ VECTOR / MATRIX }	{ MONOCHROME / COLOR }	{ UNINTELLIGENT / INTELLIGENT }	
CATHODE-RAY TUBE TERMINALS	{ VECTOR / RASTER }	{ REFRESH / STORAGE }	{ MONOCHROME / COLOR }	{ UNINTELLIGENT / INTELLIGENT }

Figure 2.6 A summary of graphics display equipment

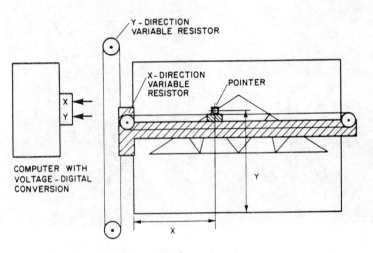

(A) Mechanical-electrical

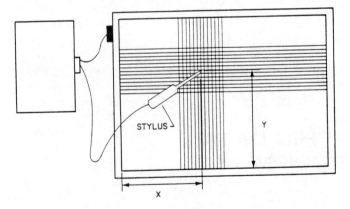

(B) Electrical-orthogonal fine wire grid

Figure 2.7 Different types of digitizing tables

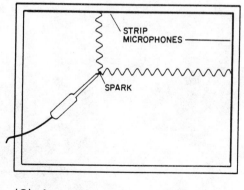

(C) Acoustic

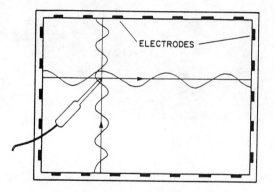

(D) Electrical-wave phase

Figure 2.7 Different types of digitizing tables (continued)

equipment can be used to input either purely graphic data or graphically prompted commands.

2.4.1 Digitizing Tables and Tablets

A digitizing table or tablet, such as is shown in Figs. 2.7 and 2.8, locates the coordinates on its surface by means of a cross-

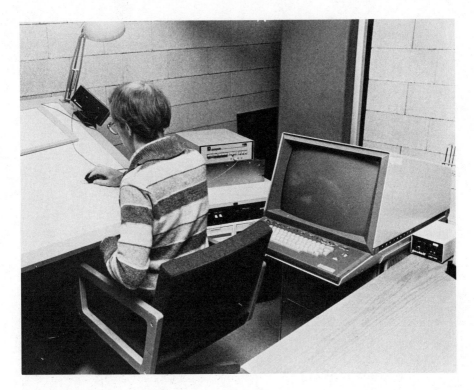

Figure 2.8 A digitizing table in use

hair intersection or the tip of a stylus positioned by the user and feeds these coordinates into the computer. The coordinates can be input into the computer in either of two modes:

1. Intermittently, under the control of the user.
2. Continuously, or in effect at very short time intervals.

By these means, boundary lines, contour lines, cross sections, building floor plans, and other engineering data can be conveniently supplied to the computer.

2.4.2 Cathode-Ray Tube Terminals

With cathode-ray tube terminals, an important distinction is again between vector and raster displays. Vector displays in-

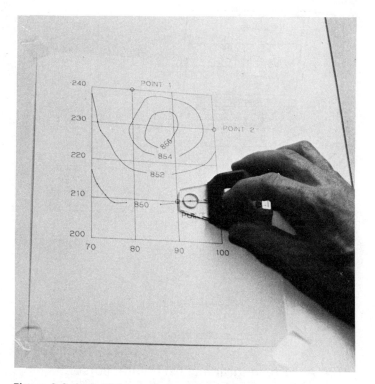

Figure 2.8 A digitizing table in use (continued)

clude both refresh and storage graphics. With refresh graphics, the "light pen" in the hands of the user functions interactively with the "cursor" or other graphic objects on the screen of the tube, at the expense of a substantial amount of computing power. With the storage tubes, the relationship between the computer and the user is much less interactive. The user positions a pair of crosshairs or a cursor and issues a command for this position to be read by the computer. Both alternatives are shown in Fig. 2.9.

2.4.3 Types of Data Input

When information is input to the computer from a CRT screen or a tablet, the data collected are the X and Y coordinates of a point located on the recording surface of the input

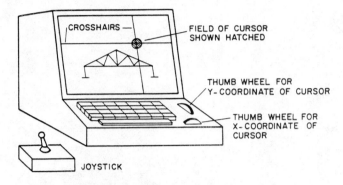

(A) A storage graphic CRT with cursor controlled by thumb wheels, joystick, or digitizing table (not shown)

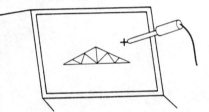

(B) A refresh graphic CRT with cursor controlled by light pen or digitizing table (not
shown)

Figure 2.9 Data input for storage and refresh graphic
CRT terminals

device. How this information is to be interpreted depends
upon the computer program being executed. The data can be
interpreted as purely graphical information—for example,
points on the contour line of a map drawn to a certain scale—
or they can be interpreted as "pick" functions to make selec-
tions from a "menu" of available graphics activities.

Figure 2.10 shows schematically the working surface of a
graphic cathode-ray tube terminal. In this example, the
region to the right is devoted to a simple menu. The much
larger region to the left is the graphics working area. A point
on the screen is positioned by the intersection of the vertical
and horizontal crosshairs which are controlled by an input
device such as the set of thumbwheels located to the right.

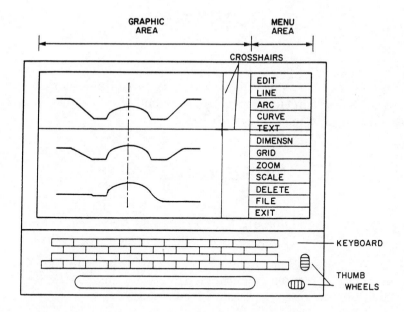

Figure 2.10 A typical screen layout for a cathode-ray
tube with graphics editor functions

When the crosshairs are in the desired position, the point
coordinates are input to the computer by pressing a key or
the space bar on the keyboard.

If the point so located falls in the graphics working area
of the screen, the program software will give the information
a graphic interpretation. However, if it lands in the menu
area, it will be interpreted as a pick from the menu. For example, if the selected point falls in the area occupied by
"LINE," the program will now expect the user to start input-
ting lines. If it falls in the area labeled "FILE," the program
will take the initial steps to file the drawing on permanent
storage.

In practice, menus can become much more elaborate
than the one shown in Fig. 2.10. In some systems, the expensive CRT screen surface is reserved for graphic information.
All the menus are handled on the digitizing table or a special
digitizing tablet. Alternatively, the menus and all nongra-
phic communication between the user and the system may be
handled on a small secondary alphanumeric screen.

SUMMARY

In this chapter, various display devices are described. A major distinction is made between display devices and input devices. A distinction between vector display devices and raster scan devices is also discussed.

REFERENCES

Newman, W. M. and Sproull, R. F., *Principles of Interactive Computer Graphics* (New York: McGraw-Hill Book Company, 1979).

Wright, Whitman, "Application of Computer Graphics in Civil Engineering," Computer Application Division, Canadian Society for Civil Engineering, Montreal, Canada, 1981.

3
RASTER
AND
RANDOM SCAN
GRAPHICS

3.1 INTRODUCTION

Raster scan and *random scan graphics* are two different methods by means of which computer-generated pictures may be drawn. Raster graphics is based upon those technologies in which an image is represented as a two-dimensional array of discrete picture elements called pixels, where each pixel has a specified intensity or color. On the other hand, random scan or vector graphics depends upon the ability of a hardware to generate line vectors. Line drawings are in most respects easier to create because the algorithms for their generation are simpler, the amount of information required to represent them is less, and they can be displayed on equipment which is more readily available. Display of line drawings is much better understood because of its application in engineering and architectural drawing. Continuous tone images or raster scan graphics could not be displayed at all until the advent in the late 1960s of the frame buffer display, and algorithms for generating these images are still being developed.

Both methods can be used to draw either an engineering drawing or a display to depict a realistic image. However, the two methods have well-defined areas of effectiveness and are used appropriately—i.e., vector graphics is used for engineering and scientific drawings, and raster graphics is used to give realism to the picture.

3.2 CLASSIFICATION OF COMPUTER GRAPHIC DEVICES

There are a number of methods of classifying computer graphic devices. Each method gives some insight into the confusing matrix of possible devices. One method of classifying the devices is according to whether they are raster scan or random scan. It may be noted that low-cost graphics will be based on microcomputer technology. This technology uses TV monitors which are raster-scan-based. In microcomputer technology, the color choice is limited, but the number of colors available is sufficient to do useful raster scan graphics.

The fundamental difference in the hardware used for the random scan or raster scan is that the random scan display device has a vector generator available. A hardware vector generator allows the drawing of lines with a minimum of data. This does not imply that a raster scan or a point-plotting device cannot be made to draw vectors by using software. A vector can, of course, be constructed as a series of points. If points are plotted close enough together, they will appear to the eye to be a solid line. All the pen plotters, storage-tube CRT devices, and refresh-tube CRT devices are random scan devices. All the TV-type CRT devices, printers, and hardcopy teletype terminals are considered to be point-plotting graphic devices.

It is essential, therefore, to distinguish between line-drawing displays and point-plotting displays. The first leads to random scan or vector graphics, and the latter leads to raster scan graphics. Because of this distinction, it should be noted that the algorithms used to display pictures or drawings will be different by two methods. However, the techniques of structuring data and storage of data are essentially independent of devices.

3.3 RASTER SCAN TECHNOLOGY

Raster scan graphics origins are traced to the simple television CRT tube, of which millions are in use around the world. In a raster scan, the image is displayed by the electron beam which follows a fixed path. This pattern is repeated about 30 times a second. An image is created by varying the intensity of the electron beam and therefore the intensity of the resulting emitted light. In simple systems, the intensity variation is between ON and OFF states, while more complex systems allow multiple levels of intensity and color.

A basic raster scan is shown in Fig. 3.1(a). Two rasters, as shown in the figure, are used to reduce flicker. The basic electrical signal used to derive the display console is an analog whose modulation represents the intensity of the individual dots which compose the picture. The CRT beam starts at the upper left of the screen and moves horizontally to the right, defining a scan line. It is during the left-to-right movement that the beam intensity is modulated. At the right edge, the beam is blanked and repositioned to the left edge, down one unit from the previous scan, as shown by the dotted line. At the end that is at the right-hand bottom corner, the beam is repositioned to the initial starting position. While North American TV operates with 525 scan lines, raster graphics systems use anywhere from 100 to 1000 scan lines.

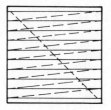

Figure 3.1(a) Raster scan pattern

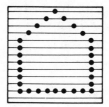

Figure 3.1(b) House displayed with raster scan

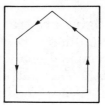

Figure 3.1(c) House displayed with random scan

On a raster display, the outline of a house would be drawn as shown in Fig. 3.1(b), which shows the scan lines and the points at which rays are intensified. The raster scan display method is completely different from the random scan display method. Figure 3.1(c) shows how the vectors are drawn to display the house. The arrows show the movement of the CRT beam in the random scan display method.

3.4 A BASIC RASTER DISPLAY SYSTEM

A basic raster display system consists of three components: the digital memory or frame buffer, the display controller, and the display monitor. A frame buffer is simply a block of digital memory in which the displayed image is stored as a matrix of intensity values. A display controller is an interface that passes the contents of the frame buffer to the monitor. The image must be passed repeatedly to the monitor, 30 or more times a second, in order to maintain a steady picture on the screen. A monitor is a television monitor—i.e., a home TV set without the tuning and receiving electronics. The relationship between the frame buffer, the display controller, and the monitor is shown in Fig. 3.2.

Inside the frame buffer, the image is stored as a pattern of binary digital numbers, which represents rectangular arrays of picture elements, or *pixels*. In the simplest case, where we wish to store only black-and-white images, we can present black pixels by 1's in the frame buffer and white pixels by 0's. Thus, a 16×16 array of black-and-white pixels could be represented by the binary values in the 32 eight-bit bytes shown in Fig. 3.2. Also, Fig. 3.3 gives more details of the frame buffer and the image on the monitor.

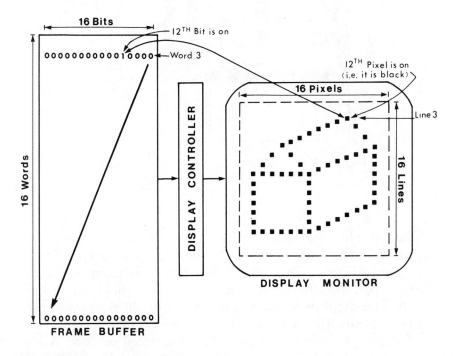

Figure 3.2 A basic raster display system

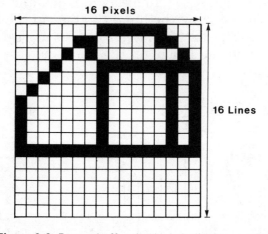

16 Bits

16 Words

16 Pixels

16 Lines

Figure 3.3 Frame buffer (top) and display monitor (bottom)

The display controller simply reads each successive byte of data from the frame buffer and converts its 0's and 1's into a corresponding *video* signal. This signal is then fed to the TV monitor, producing a black-and-white pattern on the screen. The display repeats this operation 30 times a second and thus maintains a steady picture on the TV screen.

Suppose we wish to change the displayed picture. All we

need do is modify the frame buffer's contents to represent the new pattern of pixels. In this way, we can achieve such effects as a rotating wheel that grows or shrinks.

_____ **Example**

The 16 × 16 display as shown in Fig. 3.3 uses a frame buffer of 32 bytes, or 256 bits of information. How many bits should be needed to produce an image on a TV screen with 525 scanlines (United States standard) or 625 scanlines (European standard)?

$$\text{Aspect ratio of TV} = \frac{\text{Height}}{\text{Width}} = \frac{3}{4}$$

hence,

$$\text{Number of bits for U.S.} = \frac{4}{3} \times 525 \times 525 = 367{,}500 \text{ bits or 46K bytes}$$

$$\text{Bits for Europe} = \frac{4}{3} \times 625 \times 625 = 520{,}703 \text{ bits or 65K bytes}$$

3.5 PROBLEMS IN DRAWING CURVES AND STRAIGHT LINES

The computer displays by pixels have two problems. These are:

1. Which pixel should be black and which white? The choice is not always as straightforward as one initially thinks.

2. Straight lines or curves will not be smooth in general. This usually is referred to as unpleasant *staircase* effects, as shown in Fig. 3.3(b).

The first problem is solved by using a procedure, or algorithm, that computes which pixel should be black from the equation of the line or curve. Many algorithms have been developed to indicate the state of the pixel, some of which are so simple that they can be implemented in hardware leading to very fast line and curve drawings.

The second problem, a staircase-like effect in the picture, is much more difficult to solve. The most common solution is to use a different sort of display, called a line-drawing display, which plots continuous lines and curves rather than separate pixels. With a line-drawing display, it is possible to draw lines that appear completely smooth to the unaided eye.

Until recently, line-drawing displays were the only widely used type of graphic display; the cost of digital memories made the frame buffer too expensive to consider. Although this situation is now changing, most computer graphics research has been oriented toward line-drawing displays; the frame buffer and its effective use are relatively unexplored topics.

3.6 COLOR AND GREY LEVEL RASTER DISPLAY SYSTEM

Two intensity images—i.e., 0's and 1's—are adequate for some applications, but grossly unsatisfactory for others. Additional control over the intensity of each pixel is obtained by storing more than one bit of information for each pixel. Thus, two bits yields four intensities, and so on. The bits can be used to control the color of a pixel.

Five or six bits are needed per pixel to produce a continuous shade of grey for an image. For color, fifteen to eighteen bits are needed to project each primary red, green, or blue color. For each primary, five to six bits are needed.

Raster scan systems with fifteen to eighteen bits per pixel are still relatively expensive, despite the dramatic decreases in the cost of memories. Therefore, an image display system of many raster displays includes a so-called "video look-up table." A pixel's value is not routed directly to the display monitor, but is used instead as an index into the look-up table. The table entry value is used to derive the display. For instance, with 8 bits per pixel, the table would have $2^8 =$ 256 entries. A pixel value of 67 would cause the contents of table location 67 to be used for display. This look-up operation is done for each pixel and each display cycle, so the table must be quickly accessible.

Commercially available systems typically use look-up tables with 256 entries of 12 bits each, while 24-bit entries are now becoming available. For color use, the bits are evenly divided to control red, green, and blue electron guns of the display monitor. The computer interface now accesses the image display system, not only to start and stop the display but also to load the look-up table.

SUMMARY

In this chapter, vector graphics and raster scan graphics are described. Some comments are made about a classification of computer graphic devices. Basic raster scan technology is explained in terms of frame buffer, display controller, and display monitor. Some of the problems in drawing curves and straight lines in raster scan graphics are briefly discussed.

REFERENCES

Newman, W. M. and Sproull, R. F., *Principles of Interactive Computer Graphics* (New York: McGraw-Hill Book Company, 1979).

Status Report of the Graphics Standards Committee, *Computer Graphics,* Vol. 13, No. 3, August 1979.

4
BASIC
COORDINATE GEOMETRY
IN
COMPUTER GRAPHICS

4.1 POINTS, LINES, AND PLANES

We begin our mathematical study of points, lines, and planes by defining representation of a point. A point can be represented by its coordinates. In two dimensions, these coordinate values can be specified as the elements of a row $[x \ y]$, and in three dimensions these coordinate values can be specified as the elements of a row $[x \ y \ z]$. Conversely, a transpose of a row which is a column will be admissible. Therefore, in two dimensions, a point may be represented by a column $\begin{Bmatrix} x \\ y \end{Bmatrix}$

or for three-dimensional representation could be $\begin{Bmatrix} x \\ y \\ z \end{Bmatrix}$. A series of points, each of which is a position vector, may be stored in a computer as a matrix of numbers.

A line can be drawn and defined by specifying two points as shown in Fig. 4.1. Equation of a line is given by

$$Ax + By + C = 0 \tag{4.1}$$

where A, B, and C are constants and depend upon the coordinates of two specified points. To find these constants, we use rules applying to two similar triangles, shown in Fig. 4.1.

$$\frac{x - x_1}{y - y_1} = \frac{x_2 - x_1}{y_2 - y_1}$$

or

$$(x - x_1)(y_2 - y_1) = (y - y_1)(x_2 - x_1)$$

this gives

$$x(y_2 - y_1) - y(x_2 - x_1) - (x_1y_2 - x_2y_1) = 0 \tag{4.2}$$

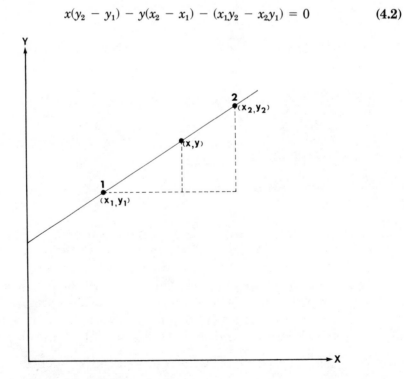

Figure 4.1 Definition of a line

Comparing equations (4.1) and (4.2), we have

$$A = (y_2 - y_1)$$
$$B = -(x_2 - x_1)$$
$$C = -(x_1 y_2 - x_2 y_1)$$

(4.3)

Alternatively, the equation of a line could be defined in terms of a determinant, as shown:

$$\begin{vmatrix} x & x_1 & x_2 \\ y & y_1 & y_2 \\ 1 & 1 & 1 \end{vmatrix} = 0$$

which gives the same result as equation (4.2) on evaluation.

$$x(y_2 - y_1) - y(x_2 - x_1) - (x_1 y_2 - x_2 y_1) = 0$$

Equation of a plane, shown in Fig. 4.2, is given by

$$Ax + By + Cz + D = 0$$

(4.4)

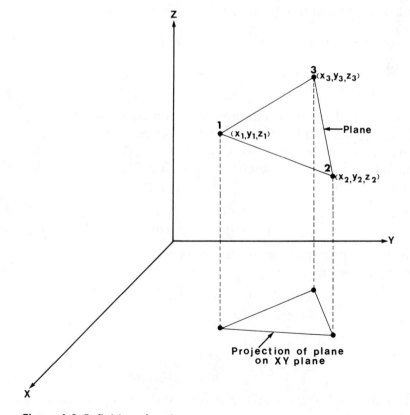

Figure 4.2 Definition of a plane

where A, B, C, and D are constants and are uniquely determined by three non-colinear points giving the following general determinant:

$$\begin{vmatrix} x & x_1 & x_2 & x_3 \\ y & y_1 & y_2 & y_3 \\ z & z_1 & z_2 & z_3 \\ 1 & 1 & 1 & 1 \end{vmatrix} = 0$$

Expansion of this determinant and comparing the terms for x, y, and z with equation (4.4) gives constants A, B, C, and D.

4.2 INTERSECTION OF TWO LINES

A study of intersection of two lines is important for development of algorithms which can be used in

(i)   Hidden line removal

(ii)   Clipping

(iii)   Area filling

Let line 1 be constructed from joining two points $[x_1 \ y_1]_1$ and $[x_2 \ y_2]_1$ and line 2 from joining points $[x_1 \ y_1]_2$ and $[x_2 \ y_2]_2$, where outer subscripts represent the line number. Using equation (4.1) to find the equation of line 1 and line 2, we find that these are

$$A_1 x + B_1 y + C_1 = 0 \qquad (4.5a)$$
$$A_2 x + B_2 y + C_2 = 0 \qquad (4.5b)$$

Hence, by multiplying equation (4.5b) by A_1, and equation (4.5a)by A_2 we get

$$A_1 A_2 x + A_2 B_1 y + A_2 C_1 = 0$$
$$A_1 A_2 x + A_1 B_2 y + A_1 C_2 = 0$$

or

$$y = -\frac{A_2 C_1 - A_1 C_2}{A_2 B_1 - A_1 B_2}$$

and by multiplying equation (4.5b) by B_1, and equation (4.5a) by B_2 we get

$$B_2A_1x + B_2B_1y + B_2C_1 = 0$$
$$B_1A_2x + B_1B_2y + B_1C_2 = 0$$

or

$$x = -\frac{B_2C_1 - B_1C_2}{B_2A_1 - B_1A_2}$$

Therefore, to find the intersection of two lines we use

$$x = -\frac{B_2C_1 - B_1C_2}{B_2A_1 - B_1A_2} \qquad \textbf{(4.6a)}$$

$$y = -\frac{A_2C_1 - A_1C_2}{A_2B_1 - A_1B_2} \qquad \textbf{(4.6b)}$$

where $A, B,$ and C could be calculated from equations (4.3) for both lines.

For example, to find the intersection of two lines whose end coordinates are:

Line 1: $x_1 = 1 \qquad y_1 = 2$
$ x_2 = 2 \qquad y_2 = 3$

and

Line 2: $x_1 = 2 \qquad y_1 = 2$
$ x_2 = 3 \qquad y_2 = 1$

using these coordinates and equation (4.3), $A, B,$ and C for line 1 are

$$A_1 = 1, B_1 = -1, C_1 = 1$$

and for line 2 are

$$A_2 = -1, B_2 = -1, C_2 = 4$$

Hence, the coordinates of the intersection point are

$$x = -\frac{-1 + 4}{-1 - 1}$$

$$= 1.5$$

and

$$y = -\frac{-1 - 4}{+1 + 1}$$

$$= 2.5$$

Whereas the lines intersect, the segments that define the cross do not. This is shown in Fig. 4.3, where the point represented by the cross has the coordinates [1.5, 2.5].

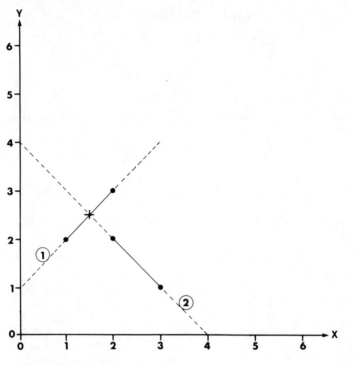

Figure 4.3 Intersection of two lines

We will be interested in the actual representation of segments rather than the intersection of the infinite lines defined by these segments.

For us to find the intersection of segments, we must investigate all possible cases that can occur when two non-parallel lines are drawn. There are three possible cases:

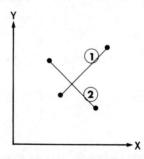

Figure 4.4(a) Line segments actually intersect

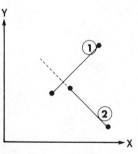

Figure 4.4(b) Apparent intersection on segment 1 but not on segment 2

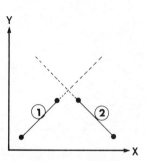

Figure 4.4(c) Apparent intersection not on either segment

To simplify the problem of determining whether or not the intersection is real or apparent, we formulate another form of the equation of a straight line.

4.2.1 Parametric Equation of a Line

Let a line be defined by two points $[x_1\, y_1]$ and $[x_2\, y_2]$, as shown in Fig. 4.5.

We define the coordinates of a point on this line as

$$x_\alpha = x_1 + T_\alpha\,(x_2 - x_1) \tag{4.7a}$$

$$y_\alpha = y_1 + T_\alpha\,(y_2 - y_1) \tag{4.7b}$$

If $(0 \leq T_\alpha \leq 1)$ is true for T_α, then the point $[x_\alpha\, y_\alpha]$ lies on the line segment.

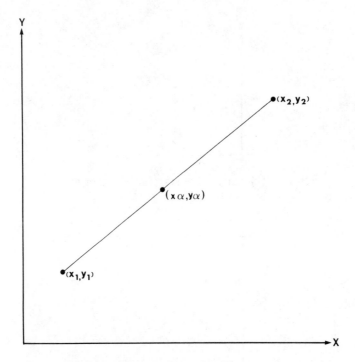

Figure 4.5 Parametric equation of a line

For

$$T_\alpha = 1, x_\alpha = x_2, \text{ and } y_\alpha = y_2$$

and for

$$T_\alpha = 0, x_\alpha = x_1, \text{ and } y_\alpha = y_1$$

Thus, if $T_\alpha < 0$ or $T_\alpha > 1$, then x_α and y_α will be beyond the segment.

We will now consider the intersection of two lines (Fig. 4.6) defined by parametric equations (4.7a) and (4.7b).

If the intersection does occur, then

$$x_\alpha = x_\beta \qquad\qquad \text{(4.8a)}$$

and

$$y_\alpha = y_\beta \qquad\qquad \text{(4.8b)}$$

Using equations (4.7a) and (4.8a), we have

$$x_1 + T_\alpha (x_2 - x_1) = x_3 + T_\beta (x_4 - x_3)$$

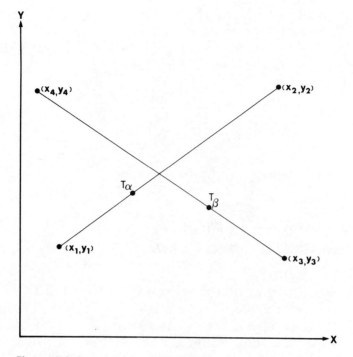

Figure 4.6 Intersection of two lines

and using equations (4.7b) and (4.8b), we have

$$y_1 + T_\alpha (y_2 - y_1) = y_3 + T_\beta (y_4 - y_3)$$

Rearranging terms,

$$(x_2 - x_1)T_\alpha - (x_4 - x_3)T_\beta = x_3 - x_1$$

$$(y_2 - y_1)T_\alpha - (y_4 - y_3)T_\beta = y_3 - y_1$$

The solution of these simultaneous equations is

$$T_\alpha = \frac{-(x_3 - x_1)(y_4 - y_3) + (y_3 - y_1)(x_4 - x_3)}{-(x_2 - x_1)(y_4 - y_3) + (y_2 - y_1)(x_4 - x_3)} \qquad \text{(4.9a)}$$

and

$$T_\beta = \frac{(x_2 - x_1)(y_3 - y_1) - (y_2 - y_1)(x_3 - x_1)}{-(x_2 - x_1)(y_4 - y_3) + (y_2 - y_1)(x_4 - x_3)} \qquad \text{(4.9b)}$$

If the denominator of the expression defining T_α and T_β is zero, then the lines are parallel. Hence, they do not intersect. If $0 \le T_\alpha \le 1$ and $0 \le T_\beta \le 1$, then the segments do intersect.

To illustrate this concept, we test equations (4.9a) and (4.9b) on the lines shown in Fig. 4.3.

$$T_\alpha = \frac{-2+1}{-2} = \frac{1}{2}$$

$$T_\beta = \frac{-1-2}{-2} = 1\frac{1}{2}$$

Hence, the segments do not intersect.

4.2.2 Program to Find Intersection of Two Lines

The following program draws and tests whether two lines intersect. An example of three lines defining a triangle and a line is used to check the results from the program. Figure 4.7(a) shows a triangle and a line. Figure 4.7(b) shows data and user messages corresponding to Fig. 4.7(a).

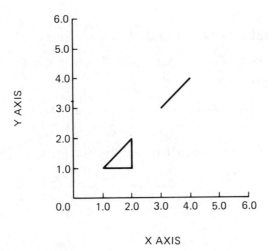

Figure 4.7(a) Intersection of lines

```
      PROGRAM INTCN (INPUT,OUTPUT,TAPE1)
C
C******************************************************************
C THIS PROGRAM DRAWS A TRIANGLE AND A LINE. THEN PROGRAM *
C CHECKS IF ANY SIDE OF THE TRIANGLE AND GIVEN LINE       *
C INTERSECTS OR NOT. LOCAL PLOTTING SOFTWARE USED AT      *
C TECHNICAL UNIVERSITY OF NOVA SCOTIA, HALIFAX, IS USED   *
C TO DRAW GRAPHICS DISPLAY. SUBROUTINE 'TEST' ANS 'BTEST'*
C ARE WRITTEN USING ALGORITHM DERIVED IN SECT. 4.2.1 .   *
C******************************************************************
C
C DECLARE NECESSARY DIMENSIONS AND DATA FOR GRAPHICS OUTPUT
C
      DIMENSION X(5) , Y(5)
      DATA NXAXIS/6HX AXIS/
      DATA NYAXIS/6HY AXIS/
C
C READ VERTICES OF A TRIANGLE.
C
      READ * , ( (X(I) , Y(I)), I = 1 , 3 )
C
C READ VERTICES OF A LINE
C
      READ * , ( (X(I) , Y(I)), I = 4 , 5 )
C
C INVOKE PLOTTING ROUTINES AND DRAW X AND Y AXIS
C
      CALL INITAL(1,100,11,0)
      CALL PLOT(2.0,2.0,-3)
      CALL AXIS(0.0,0.0,NXAXIS,-6,6.0,0.0,0.0,1.0,1)
      CALL AXIS(0.0,0.0,NYAXIS,6,6.0,90.0,0.0,1.0,1)
C
C DRAW TRIANGLE AND LINE
C
      CALL PLOT(X(1),Y(1),3)
      CALL PLOT(X(2),Y(2),2)
      CALL PLOT(X(3),Y(3),2)
      CALL PLOT(X(1),Y(1),2)
      CALL PLOT(X(4),Y(4),3)
      CALL PLOT(X(5),Y(5),2)
C
C TERMINATE PLOTTING AND CALL SUBROUTINE 'TEST' TO CHECK
C INTERSECTION OF ANY SIDE OF A TRINAGLE AND GIVEN LINE.
C
      CALL PENUP
      CALL RSTR(2)
C
      CALL TEST(X(1),Y(1),X(2),Y(2),X(4),Y(4),X(5),Y(5),N1)
      CALL TEST(X(1),Y(1),X(3),Y(3),X(4),Y(4),X(5),Y(5),N2)
      CALL TEST(X(2),Y(2),X(3),Y(3),X(4),Y(4),X(5),Y(5),N3)
C
C FOR INTERSECTION N1, N2, AND N3 ARE EQUAL TO 1 . CHECK FOR
C POSSIBLE INTERSECTION AND PRINT APPROPRIATE MESSAGE.
C
      IF( (N1.EQ.0) .AND. (N2.EQ.0) .AND. (N3.EQ.0) ) PRINT 5
      STOP
    5 FORMAT(//,10X,*GIVEN LINE DOES NOT INTERSECT TRIANGLE*,10(/))
      END
```

```
          SUBROUTINE TEST(X1,Y1,X2,Y2,X3,Y3,X4,Y4,N)
C
C*********************************************************************
C  THIS SUBROUTINE CHECKS, USING ALGORITHM OF SECT.4.2.1,   *
C  THAT TWO LINES WITH GIVEN CO-ORDINATES INTERSECTS OR NOT*
C*********************************************************************
C
C  CALCULATE DENOMINATOR. IF DENOMINATOR IS 0.0 THEN LINES ARE
C  PARALLEL. CALL SUBROUTINE BTEST TO CHECK IF THEY COINSIDE
C  OR NOT. OTHERWISE MAKE FURTHER TESTS FOR INTERSECTION OF
C  LINES. SET FLAG FOR NO INTERSECTION ( N = 0 ) .
C
          N = 0
          DENOM = ( (Y2-Y1) * (X4-X3) ) - ( (X2-X1) * (Y4-Y3) )
          IF ( DENOM .EQ. 0.0 ) GO TO 10
          TALPHA = ( ( (Y3-Y1)*(X4-X3) ) - ( (X3-X1)*(Y4-Y3) ) ) / DENOM
          TBETA  = ( ( (X2-X1)*(Y3-Y1) ) - ( (Y2-Y1)*(X3-X1) ) ) / DENOM
          IF ( (TALPHA .LT. 0.0 ) .OR. (TALPHA .GT. 1.0 ) ) RETURN
          IF ( (TBETA .LT. 0.0 ) .OR. (TBETA .GT. 1.0 ) ) RETURN
          N = 1
          PRINT 15 , X1,Y1,X2,Y2
          RETURN
C
C  CALL SUBROUTINE 'BTEST'
C
   10 CALL BTEST(X1,Y1,X2,Y2,X3,Y3,N1)
          CALL BTEST(X1,Y1,X2,Y2,X4,Y4,N2)
          IF ( (N1.NE.0) .OR. (N2.NE.0) ) RETURN
          PRINT 20
          RETURN
C
   15 FORMAT(//,10X,*LINE INTERSECTS TRIANGLE SIDE*,4(2X,F5.2),//)
   20 FORMAT(//,10X,*LINE PARALLEL TO ONE SIDE BUT NO INTERSECTION*,/)
          END




          SUBROUTINE BTEST(X1,Y1,X2,Y2,X3,Y3,L)
C
C*********************************************************************
C                                                                   *
C  THIS SUBROUTINE CHECKS IF TWO PARALLEL LINES COINSIDE OR NOT  *
C                                                                   *
C*********************************************************************
C
          L = 0
          IF ( (X2-X1) .NE. 0.0 ) GO TO 5
          WRITE 15
          RETURN
    5 TALPHA = ( X3 - X1 ) / ( X2 - X1 )
          IF ( ( TALPHA .LT. 0.0 ) .OR. ( TALPHA .GT. 1.0 ) ) RETURN
          L = 1
          WRITE 10
          RETURN
   10 FORMAT(//,10X,*LINE COINSIDE WITH ONE SIDE OF TRIANGLE*,/)
   15 FORMAT(//,10X,*WRONG CO-ORDINATES OF A SIDE OF TRIANGLE*,/)
          END
```

DATA FILE

1.0 1.0
2.0 1.0
2.0 2.0
3.0 3.0
4.0 4.0

USER MESSAGES

LINE PARALLEL TO ONE SIDE BUT NO INTERSECTION

GIVEN LINE DOES NOT INTERSECT TRIANGLE

Figure 4.7(b) Data and user messages corresponding
to Fig. 4.7(a)

4.3 VECTORS,
SCALAR PRODUCT,
AND CROSS PRODUCT

A vector has direction and magnitude. The magnitude of a
vector is calculated from the end points of the vector, and
directions are usually specified in the Cartesian coordinates
by the unit vectors i, j, and k.

Let vector $V_1 [x_1 \, y_1]$ and $V_2 [x_2 \, y_2]$ be defined by $x_1, y_1, x_2,$
and y_2 (Fig. 4.8), where $x_1, y_1, x_2,$ and y_2 are differences between
the end coordinates of the vectors V_1 and V_2.

We can find a new vector V as

$$V = V_1 - V_2 = [(x_1 - x_2)(y_1 - y_2)]$$

The scalar or dot product of vectors is defined as

$$V_1 \cdot V_2 = |V_1| \, |V_2| \cos \theta = x_1 x_2 + y_1 y_2$$

where $|V_1|$ and $|V_2|$ are the lengths of vectors V_1 and V_2. The
lengths are given by the following formulas

$$|V_1| = \sqrt{x_1^2 + y_1^2}$$
$$|V_2| = \sqrt{x_2^2 + y_2^2}$$

(4.10)

and $\cos \theta$ = cosine of the angle between the two vectors. It is
noted that the dot product is a scalar quantity—that is, it
has only a magnitude.

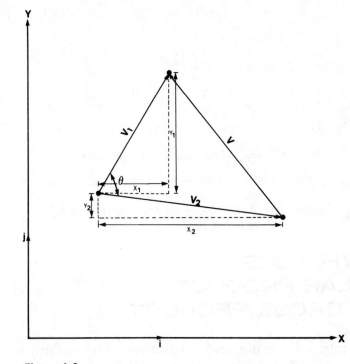

Figure 4.8

The cross product of two vectors is determined by

$$V_1 \times V_2 = \begin{vmatrix} i & j & k \\ x_1 & y_1 & 0 \\ x_2 & y_2 & 0 \end{vmatrix}$$

If we expand the determinant using minors, we get

$$V_1 \times V_2 = k(x_1 y_2 - x_2 y_1) \tag{4.11}$$

The cross product of two vectors V_1 and V_2 is also a vector and is perpendicular to the plane containing vectors V_1 and V_2. The cross product is often used to define the equation of a plane containing the vectors V_1 and V_2.

4.3.1 Equation of a Plane Using Vectors

If we are given three non-colinear points in a plane (as shown in Fig. 4.2), we can construct two vectors, say V_1 and V_2, given as follows:

$$V_1 = (x_2 - x_1)i + (y_2 - y_1)j + (z_2 - z_1)k$$
$$V_2 = (x_3 - x_1)i + (y_3 - y_1)j + (z_3 - z_1)k$$

We take the cross product of V_1 and V_2. This product gives a normal to the plane. The constants A, B, and C are then defined as

$$A = (y_2 - y_1)(z_3 - z_1) - (y_3 - y_1)(z_2 - z_1)$$
$$B = (x_2 - x_1)(z_3 - z_1) + (x_3 - x_1)(z_2 - z_1)$$
$$C = (x_2 - x_1)(y_3 - y_1) - (x_3 - x_1)(y_2 - y_1)$$

Once A, B, and C are determined, we use the equation of the plane $Ax + By + Cz + D = 0$ and a given point to find the last constant D.

4.4 FAST DRAWING OF CURVES

In the past, the functions were calculated by defining the expressions. Although this method is accurate, it seems to utilize a considerable amount of CPU time for the drawing of curves. The alternate procedure of drawing curves, which is much more efficient but not as accurate, is explained below.

4.4.1 Quadratic Curve

Suppose we have the equation

$$y = ax^2 + bx + c$$

We want to plot y as a function of x for equally spaced values of $x = 0, 1, 2, 3 \ldots$. The first derivative $\dfrac{dy}{dx}$ near i is given by

$$\left(\frac{dy}{dx}\right)_i \doteq \frac{y_{i+1} - y_i}{\Delta x} = \frac{\Delta y}{\Delta x}$$

where

Δy = first difference of the function, and

Δx = step

and

$$\left(\frac{dy}{dx}\right)_{i+1} \doteq \frac{y_{i+2} - y_{i+1}}{\Delta x}$$

and the second derivative near i is given by

$$\left(\frac{dy^2}{dx^2}\right)_i \doteq \frac{\dfrac{y_{i+2} - y_{i+1}}{\Delta x} - \dfrac{y_{i+1} - y_i}{\Delta x}}{\Delta x}$$

$$\doteq \frac{y_{i+2} - 2y_{i+1} + y_i}{\Delta x^2}$$

$$\doteq \frac{\Delta_y^2}{\Delta x^2}$$

where Δ_y^2 = second difference. It should be noted that for a quadratic function, Δ_y^2 will be a constant quantity. Therefore we need only to evaluate y for the first three values and the remaining values of y can be determined by simple addition. This procedure to compute y will save considerable amount of CPU time in plotting curves.

For example:

$$y = 10x^2 + 3x + 2$$

Let

Δ_y as the first difference = $y_{i+1} - y_i$

Δ_y^2 as the second difference = $y_{i+2} - 2y_{i+1} + y_i$

i = 1, 2, 3

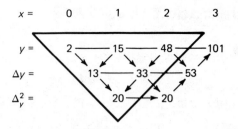

A simple program for calculating the differences is as follows. Assume we calculate the first three values of y from the function definition. Using these values, we can calculate Δy and Δ_y^2 the first and second difference. Now let y be the function we are evaluating. Let y_1 be the first difference. Let y_2 be the second difference.

We start with the following initial conditions:

$$y = y_3$$
$$y_1 = \Delta y$$
$$y_2 = \Delta_y^2$$

```
DO LOOP I = 4, . . .
      Y₁ = Y₁ + Y₂
      Y = Y + Y₁
LOOP CONTINUE
```

This program generates the values of y. For example, the fourth value of y will be found as shown below.

$$\left. \begin{array}{l} y = y_3 = 48 \\ y_1 = y = 33 \\ y_2 = 20 \end{array} \right\} \rightarrow \text{starting values}$$

$$y_1 = y_1 + y_2 = 33 + 20 = 53$$
$$y = y + y_1 = 48 + 53 = 101$$

4.4.2 Cubic Curve

To give another example, we evaluate a cubic function.

$$y = 3x^3 - 2x^2 + 6x + 5$$

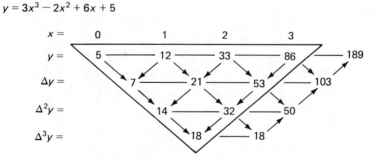

For a cubic, the third difference is a constant.
Let

y be the function,

y_1 be the first difference,

y_2 be the second difference, and

y_3 be the third difference.

Define initial values.

$$y = y \ \ = 86$$
$$y_1 = \Delta y = 53$$
$$y_2 = \Delta_y^2 = 32$$
$$y_3 = \Delta_y^3 = \text{constant} = 18$$

```
DO LOOP I = 5, . . .
    Y₂ = Y₂ + Y₃
    Y₁ = Y₁ + Y₂
    Y = Y + Y₁
LOOP CONTINUE.
```

4.4.3 Fast Calculation for a Circle

We can construct an algorithm to calculate coordinates of a circle by using the following formulation and Fig. 4.9.

Let

$$x_{i+1} = x_i + \Delta x$$

and

$$y_{i+1} = y_i + \Delta y$$

then

$$\Delta x = - (R\Delta\theta) \sin \theta = -R \sin \theta \Delta\theta = -y_i \Delta\theta$$
$$\Delta y = \ \ (R\Delta\theta) \cos \theta = \ \ R \cos \theta \Delta\theta = x_i \Delta\theta$$
$$x_{i+1} = x_i - \Delta\theta y_i$$
$$y_{i+1} = y_i + \Delta\theta x_i$$
$$\begin{Bmatrix} x_{i+1} \\ y_{i+1} \end{Bmatrix} = \begin{bmatrix} 1 & -\Delta\theta \\ \Delta\theta & 1 \end{bmatrix} \begin{Bmatrix} x_i \\ y_i \end{Bmatrix}$$

Let N and R be two vectors in the normal and radial directions.

$$N = \{-y_i\Delta\theta, x_i\Delta\theta\}$$
$$R = \{x_i, y_i\}$$

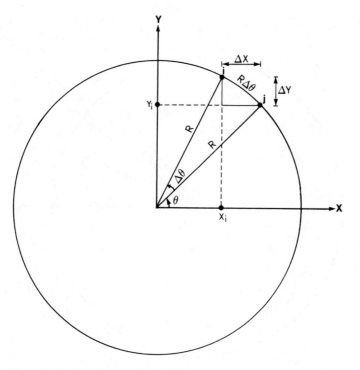

Figure 4.9 Calculation of a circle

Check to see if N and R are perpendicular.

$$N.R = -x_iy_i\Delta\theta + x_iy_i\Delta\theta = 0$$

Also note that the determinant of the transformation matrix is greater than 1—i.e.,

$$1 + \Delta\theta^2 > 1 \text{ even for small } \Delta\theta$$

We see from Fig. 4.10 that each successive point lies further from the circle. This is from the fact that the determinant is >1, which means that applying the transformation over and over again will increase the length of the vectors. Therefore, we modify the matrix as follows:

$$\begin{Bmatrix} x_{i+1} \\ y_{i+1} \end{Bmatrix} = \begin{bmatrix} 1 & -\Delta\theta \\ \Delta\theta & 1 - \Delta\theta^2 \end{bmatrix} \begin{Bmatrix} x_i \\ y_i \end{Bmatrix}$$

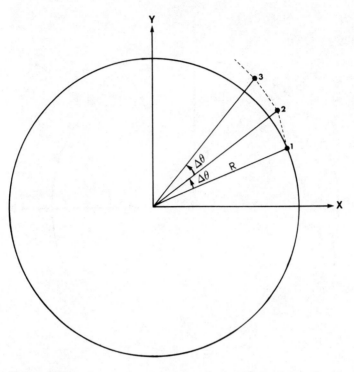

Figure 4.10

This gives the determinant of the matrix as unity.

$$x_{i+1} = x_i - y_i\Delta\theta$$
$$y_{i+1} = x_i\Delta\theta + (1 - \Delta\theta^2)y_i$$
$$= x_i\Delta\theta + y_i - \Delta\theta^2 y_i$$
$$= y_i + \Delta\theta(x_i - \Delta\theta y_i)$$
$$y_{i+1} = y_i + \Delta\theta x_{i+1}$$

Hence,

$$x_{i+1} = x_i - \Delta\theta y_i$$
$$y_{i+1} = y_i + \Delta\theta x_{i+1}$$

If $\Delta\theta$ is a power of 2, then the multiplication can be reduced to a shift.

_____ **Note:**

Shift operation is approximately twice as fast as the add arithmetic operation.

4.5 CONSIDERATIONS OF CPU TIME AND ACCURACY

Let us consider the quadratic curve for the analysis if y was calculated by the formula

$$y = 10x^2 + 3x + 2$$

Suppose we are given CDC 6400 Central Processing Unit (CPU) time for different operations.

$$\text{Add and subtract} = 11 \text{ minor cycles}$$
$$\text{Multiply and divide} = 57 \text{ minor cycles}$$
$$\text{Exponentiation} = \text{exponent} \times \text{multiply time}$$

Hence, in our calculations per point using formula,

$$
\begin{aligned}
\text{Addition} &= 2 \times 11 = && 22 \\
\text{Multiplication} &= 2 \times 57 = && 114 \\
\text{Exponentiation} &= 1 \times 57 = && \underline{57} \\
& && 193 \text{ minor cycles}
\end{aligned}
$$

where

$$
\begin{aligned}
\text{minor cycle} &= 100 \text{ N second} \\
&= 100 \times 10^{-9} = 10^{-7} \text{ s}
\end{aligned}
$$

Hence,

$$\text{CPU}_f \text{ time} = 193 \times 10^{-7} \times n$$

where
$$\text{CPU}_f = \text{CPU time using formula method}$$
$$n = \text{number of points}$$

Now for the difference formula:

(a) Calculate 3 points by formula $= 3 \times 193 = 579 \times 10^{-7}$

(b) Calculate differences first $\quad = 2 \times \quad 11 = \quad 22 \times 10^{-7}$

(c) Calculate differences second $= 1 \times \quad 11 = \quad \underline{11 \times 10^{-7}}$
$$612 \times 10^{-7}$$

$$
\begin{aligned}
\text{CPU}_d &= 612 \times 10^{-7} + 2 \times 11 \times 10^{-7} \times n \\
&= 612 \times 10^{-7} + 22 \times 10^{-7} \times n
\end{aligned}
$$

where CPU_d = CPU time using difference method

$$\frac{\mathrm{CPU}_d}{\mathrm{CPU}_f} = \frac{612 \times 10^{-7} + 22 \times 10^{-7} \times N}{193 \times 10^{-7} \times N}$$

$$= \frac{633 + 22n}{193n}$$

$$= \frac{633}{193n} + \frac{22}{193}$$

Substituting for $n = 1000$, the difference approach is 9 times faster.

Although we gain on the CPU time, we lose on accuracy. Therefore, the calculation must be done in high precision. For example, assume we are going to calculate 4096 (2^{12}) values of y to an accuracy of 8 bits. Consider the case for the quadratic; assume a 1-bit error in calculation of $\Delta^2 y$. This error propagates 2^{12} times during the calculation of Δy, and 2^{24} for the calculation of y. Thus, to calculate an 8-bit value of y 4096 times requires at least a 32-bit word, 24 bits for error and 8 bits for data.

4.6 PROGRAM TO COMPARE DIFFERENCE METHOD AND FORMULA OF A CIRCLE

We consider now an example which draws a circle with its center at the origin, employing the difference approach and traditional formula using 10, 100, and 1000 segments per quadrant of the circle $R = 3$ in. We compare the time taken to draw a circle with the traditional formula of a circle ($x^2 + y^2 = 9$) and the difference approach.

A program circle is written to compare the two methods. This program calls on a series of subprograms from the computer library for plotting. The program is written in FOR-TRAN language and was implemented on Control Data Cor-

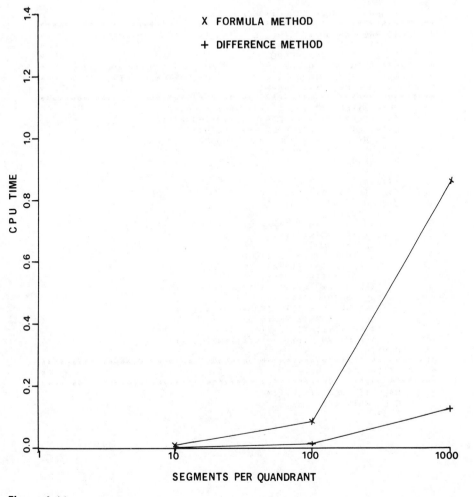

Figure 4.11

poration's Cyber 170 computer. It will be clear from Fig. 4.11 which shows segments versus time, that the difference approach is much faster than the traditional method. The program is structured and extensively commented to be easily understood.

```
      PROGRAM CIRCLE (INPUT,OUTPUT,TAPE1)
*********************************************************************
*    THIS PROGRAM DRAWS CIRCLES USING TWO DIFFERENT METHODS        *
*         1)   THE FORMULA METHOD                                  *
*         2)   THE DIFFERENCE METHOD                               *
*    THREE SETS OF CIRCLES ARE DRAWN USING 10, 100, AND 1000       *
*    SEGMENTS PER QUADRANT. THE CPU TIME FOR EACH METHOD IS        *
*    THEN COMPARED ON A GRAPH.                                     *
*********************************************************************
      REAL TIMED(3),TIMEF(3),X(4000),Y(4000)
      INTEGER IPOINT(3),METHOD1(2),METHOD2(2)
      DATA METHOD1/"DIFFERENCE"," METHOD"/
      DATA METHOD2/"FORMULA ME","THOD"/
      DATA IPOINT/10,100,1000/
      RADIUS=30.0
      X(1)=RADIUS
      Y(1)=0.
      CALL INITAL(1,100,11,0)
      CALL PLOT(0.,5.,-3)
      DO 10 I=1,3
         RAN=8.0*ATAN(1.0)/(FLOAT(IPOINT(I))*4.)
         IEND=4*IPOINT(I)-1
         CALL SECOND(TIME1)
         CALL DIFF (X,Y,IEND,RAN)
         CALL SECOND (TIME2)
         TIMED(I)=TIME2-TIME1
         CALL DRAWW (X,Y,IPOINT(I),METHOD1)
         CALL SECOND (TIME1)
         CALL FORMULA (X,Y,IEND,RAN,RADIUS)
         CALL SECOND (TIME2)
         TIMEF(I)=TIME2-TIME1
         CALL DRAWW (X,Y,IPOINT(I),METHOD2)
 10   CONTINUE
*********************************************************************
*    PLOT THE TIME GRAPH                                           *
*********************************************************************
      CALL TIMEPLT(TIMEF,TIMED)
      CALL RSTR (2)
      STOP
      END
```

```
      SUBROUTINE DIFF(X,Y,IEND,RAN)
*************************************************************************
*    THIS ROUTINE CALCULATES THE VALUES FOR X AND Y USING            *
*    THE DIFFERENCE METHOD                                           *
*************************************************************************
      REAL X(4000),Y(4000)
      DO 1 I=1,IEND
         X(I+1)=X(I)-Y(I)*RAN
         Y(I+1)=Y(I)+RAN*X(I+1)
    1 CONTINUE
      RETURN
      END


      SUBROUTINE FORMULA (X,Y,IEND,RAN,RADIUS)
*************************************************************************
*    THIS ROUTINE CALCULATES THE VALUES FOR X AND Y USING            *
*    THE FORMULA FOR A CIRCLE                                        *
*************************************************************************
      REAL X(4000),Y(4000)
      DO 1 I=1,IEND
         ARG=FLOAT(I)*RAN
         X(I+1)=RADIUS*COS(ARG)
         Y(I+1)=RADIUS*SIN(ARG)
    1 CONTINUE
      RETURN
      END


      SUBROUTINE DRAWW (X,Y,NPOINT,METHOD)
*************************************************************************
*    THIS ROUTINE PLOTS OUT THE CIRCLES.                             *
*************************************************************************
      DIMENSION METHOD(2),X(4000),Y(4000)
      MPOINT=NPOINT*4
      POINT=FLOAT(NPOINT)
      CALL PLOT(10.,0.,-3)
      CALL AXIS(-4.,0.," ",-1,8.,0.,-40.,10.,1)
      CALL AXIS(0.,-4.," ",1,8.,90.,-40.,10.,1)
      CALL SYMBOL(-2.,-5.,.21,METHOD,0.,20)
      CALL NUMBER(-1.25,4.5,.21,POINT,0.,-1)
      CALL SYMBOL(-.4,4.5,.21,"SEGMENTS",0.,8)
      CALL PLOT (X(1)/10.,Y(1)/10.,3)
      CALL PENDN
      DO 10 J=1,MPOINT
         CALL PLOT (X(J)/10.,Y(J)/10.,2)
   10 CONTINUE
      RETURN
      END
```

```
      SUBROUTINE TIMEPLT(TIME1,TIME2)
*****************************************************************
*    THIS ROUTINE PLOTS THE CPU TIME AGAINST THE NUMBER OF     *
*    SEGMENTS PER QUADRANT USING A SEMI-LOG GRAPH.             *
*****************************************************************
      REAL TIME1(3),TIME2(3),SEGMENT(3),POINTS(3)
      DATA POINTS/10.,100.,1000./
      CALL PLOT(10.,-4.,-3)
      CALL AXIS(0.,0.,"CPU TIME",8,8.,90.,0.,0.2,3)
      CALL LOGAXIS
      DO 10 I=1,3
         TIME1(I)=TIME1(I)*5.0
         TIME2(I)=TIME2(I)*5.0
         SEGMENT(I)=ALOG(POINTS(I))
  10  CONTINUE
*****************************************************************
*    PLOT THE LINE FOR THE FORMULA METHOD                      *
*****************************************************************
      CALL LINE(SEGMENT,TIME1,3,2,1)
*****************************************************************
*    PLOT THE LINE FOR THE DIFFERNECE METHOD                   *
*****************************************************************
      CALL LINE(SEGMENT,TIME2,3,1,1)
      CALL SYMBOL(2.,8.,.21,"X - FORMULA METHOD",0.,18)
      CALL SYMBOL(2.,7.5,.21,"+ - DIFERENCE METHOD",0.,20)
      RETURN
      END




      SUBROUTINE LOGAXIS
*****************************************************************
*    THIS ROUTINE PLOTS OUT A X LOG AXIS FOR THE SEGMENTS PER  *
*    QUADRANT VARIABLE.                                        *
*    SIZE IS THE SIZE OF THE CHARACTERS ON THE AXIS            *
*    OFF IS THE DISTANCE FROM THE TICKS THAT THE CHARACTERS    *
*        ARE PLOTTED                                           *
*    OFFSET IS THE LENGTH OF THE TICKS OFF THE AXIS            *
*****************************************************************
      REAL VALUE(3)
      DATA VALUE/10.,100.,1000./
      SIZE=.14
      OFF=.25
      OFFSET=.0625
*****************************************************************
*    PLOT THE AXIS LINE                                        *
*****************************************************************
      CALL PLOT(0.,0.,3)
      CALL PLOT(8.,0.,2)
      DO 10 I=1,3
         X=ALOG(VALUE(I))
*****************************************************************
*    PLOT THE TICKS                                            *
*****************************************************************
         CALL PLOT(X,0.,3)
         CALL PLOT(X,-OFFSET,2)
         FNUM=VALUE(I)
*****************************************************************
*    PLOT THE AXIS VALUES                                      *
*****************************************************************
         CALL NUMBER(X-.125,OFFSET-OFF,SIZE,FNUM,0.,1)
  10  CONTINUE
*****************************************************************
*    PLOT THE AXIS LABEL                                       *
*****************************************************************
      CALL SYMBOL(2.3,-.75,.14,"SEGMENTS PER QUADRANT",0.,21)
      RETURN
      END
```

SUMMARY

In this chapter, basic coordinate geometry in computer graphics, such as definitions of points, lines, and planes, is discussed. Mathematical equations for the intersection of two lines are developed. An algorithm based on the difference approach to draw curves fast is described.

Finally, two FORTRAN programs are given which employ the concepts of intersection of two lines and fast drawing of curves. Various devices are used to display the lines and curves.

REFERENCES

Jaeger, L. G., *Cartesian Tensors in Engineering Science* (London, England: Pergamon Press, 1966).

Roger, D. F. and Adam, A. J., *Mathematical Elements for Computer Graphics* (New York: McGraw-Hill Book Company, 1976).

Wolstenholme, E., *Elementary Vectors* (London, England: Pergamon Press, 1964).

5
DATA STRUCTURES
FOR
COMPUTER
GRAPHICS

5.1 INTRODUCTION

Data are structured in order to be manipulated. The type of structure depends on the manipulation desired. Conversely, the efficiency of the manipulation algorithm depends on the appropriateness of the data structure. To structure data effectively, it is essential not only to know techniques but also to know when to apply certain techniques. We present basic data manipulation: searching, sorting, and updating, and special-purpose algorithms that are linked to a particular data structure—e.g., array processing, sparse lists, and link lists. The building blocks of data structures are called primitive data types and in FORTRAN language these are:

Integer, Real, Character, and Logical

In a structural sense, these primitive data will become fields of a node, and a collection of nodes in a logical order will give us lists. When one builds a data structure out of primitive, one needs two functions:

1. A method of constructing the structure from its components. This function is called *Constructor*.

2. A method of separating the structure from its components. This function is called *Selector*.

5.2 STATIC STRUCTURE

In the computer, we place the nodes in consecutive storage locations. In a sequential data structure, each node is immediately adjacent to the next node. A list stored in contiguous locations is called a *dense list*. A dense list has no need for pointers because we can use an index to locate individual nodes. A dense list could be constructed from an array. However, FORTRAN does not provide constructors for arrays. Instead, the program begins execution with several predefined arrays already in existence. The nature of these predefined arrays is specified in the DIMENSION statement. It is impossible to construct new arrays once the program is underway. Arrays are constructed at compile time.

FORTRAN does provide selectors for arrays. They are hidden behind the subscripting operation. When an integer is used as a subscript, it can be considered to be a selector, selecting an individual element from the array according to its displacement from the beginning of the array. This kind of selector can appear on both sides of the equal sign in an assignment statement. The field provided by a selector can thus be used either as a destination in which to store a value or as a source from which to obtain a value. This is one of the important characteristics of selectors.

Arrays as a dense list are used for data structure of ob-

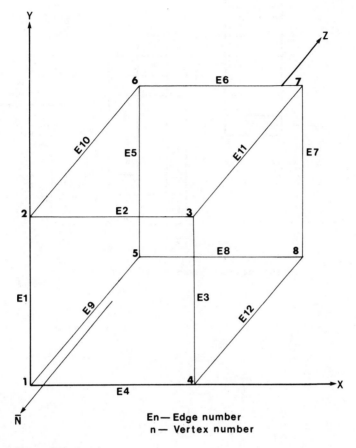

Figure 5.1 A cube

jects when these objects do not shrink, expand, or change their shape.

We consider a data structure which could be constructed for a cube, shown in Fig. 5.1, by using arrays and vectors. Four separate arrays would be needed. These are:

1. A vertex array, which keeps a list of coordinates of vertices in a cube.

2. An edge array, which points to the vertex array.

3. A surface array, which points to the edge array.

4. A normal array, which keeps directions of normals for each surface.

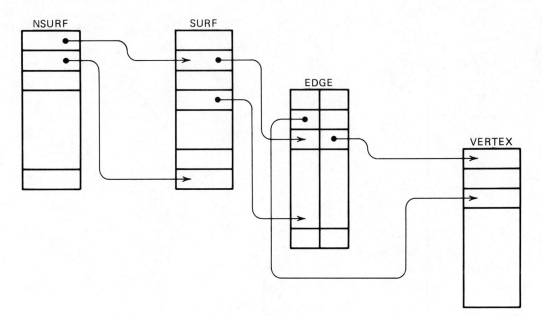

(a)   The data structure constructed from the arrays

NSURF				
	X	Y	Z	
1	0	0	−1	
2	−1	0	0	
3	0	0	1	
4	1	0	0	
5	0	−1	0	
6	0	1	0	

SURF (6, 4)			
Edge (1)	Edge (2)	Edge (3)	Edge (4)
1	2	3	4
1	9	5	10
8	7	6	5
3	11	7	12
4	12	8	9
2	11	10	6

EDGE (12 X 2)		
1	1	2
2	2	3
3	3	4
4	4	1
5	5	6
6	6	7
7	7	8
8	8	5
9	1	5
10	2	6
11	3	7
12	4	8

VERT (8 X 3)			
	x	y	z
1	0.	0.	0.
2	0.	1.	0.
3	1.	1.	0.
4	1.	0.	0.
5	0.	0.	1.
6	0.	1.	1.
7	1.	1.	1.
8	1.	0.	1.

(b)   Data structure using arrays

Figure 5.2

74

In Fig. 5.2(a), the data structure constructed from the arrays is shown. The structural relationship is indicated by pointing arrows between different arrays. This type of relationship is needed to select various types of data to draw the cube. The actual data pertaining to the cube are shown in Fig. 5.2(b).

We can easily manipulate data structured in the form of arrays. For example, if we wish to find the surface orientation of the cube, we just need to take a vector dot product.

$$V_i \cdot N_i = |V_i| \cdot |N_i| \cos \theta_i$$

Vectors V_i and N_i and angle θ_i are shown in Fig. 5.3 and refer to surfaces $i = 1, 2, 3, 4, 5, 6$. It is easy to decide whether a surface is front-facing or back-facing by inspecting angle θ. We remember that $\cos \theta_i$ is positive for $-90° < \theta < 90°$. Therefore,

(i)   The surface with normal N_i is front-facing if $|\theta_i| < 90°$.

(ii)   The surface with normal N_i is back-facing if $|\theta_i| > 90°$.

In the case of the cube shown in Fig. 5.3, N_1 is front-facing and N_2 is back-facing. Thus, the surface orientation algorithm could be used to draw only the edges of the front-facing surfaces.

(i)   If an edge is common to a front-facing and a back-facing surface, then it is an exterior edge.

(ii)   If an edge is common to two front-facing surfaces, then it is an interior edge.

(iii)   If an edge is common to two back-facing surfaces, then it is invisible.

5.3 DYNAMIC STRUCTURES

One of the structures which can grow or shrink, depending upon the usage of it, is the linearly linked list. In this approach, we use pointers or links to refer to elements of a linear list. Consider two points joining a segment as shown in

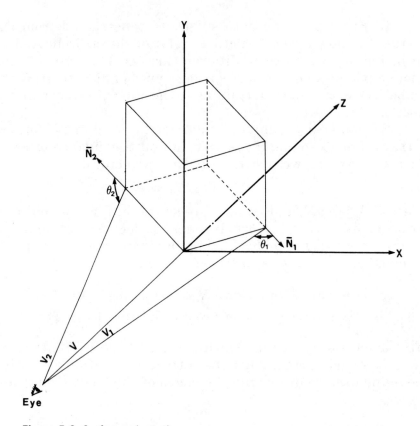

Figure 5.3 Surface orientation

Fig. 5.4. The information about the segment can be stored as a linked linear list, as shown in Fig. 5.5.

The list has two nodes. Each node has four fields; in each field, data or a pointer are stored. For example, a node in our list contains coordinates of a points, characters to distinguish its occurrence, and a pointer to the next node. Null pointer indicates that the end of a list is reached.

Now, consider that we wish to add three new vertices, as

Figure 5.4 Line segment

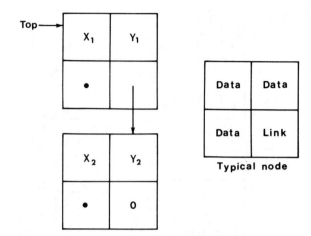

Figure 5.5 Linked linear list of a line

shown in Fig. 5.6. We will have to expand our list, as shown in Fig. 5.7.

We expanded the linked linear list in Fig. 5.7(b) from Fig. 5.7(a) by modifying links and inserting three more nodes. The insertion of nodes requires an access to an availability list from which we can obtain nodes. We also should be able to return a node to the availability list if it is no longer needed.

5.4 GENERATION OF AVAILABILITY LIST

A code is shown to generate an empty list of 1000 nodes to be used to create lists for specific functions. It is noted that the

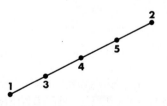

Figure 5.6 Line segments

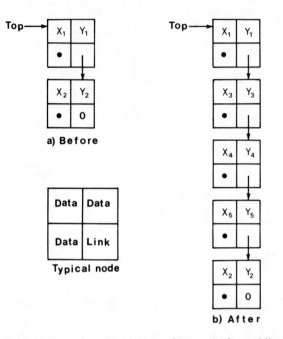

Figure 5.7 Linked linear list before and after adding new vertices to the line

declaration statements are omitted at this stage. These will be included when we arrive at coding the whole program.

```
C
C       GENERATE AVAILABILITY LIST
C
        DO 10 I = 1,999
C       FILL IN THE LINK FOR EACH NODE
10          LINK (I) = I + 1
C       FILL IN THE NULL POINTER FOR THE LAST NODE
            LINK(1000) = 0
C       INITIALIZE AVAILABLE, THE POINTER TO  THE  FREE  STORAGE
C       LIST
            AVAIL = 1
            .
            .
            .
            .
```

The list that is available to us is shown in Fig. 5.8. It is an empty list, ready to be used. Use of 1000 nodes is an arbitrary

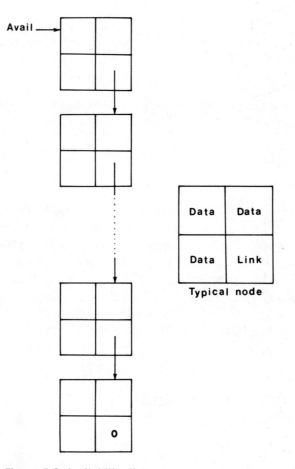

Typical node

Figure 5.8 Availability list

choice and will depend largely on the size of the list, the problem being solved, and the capacity of the computer to manipulate the list.

5.4.1 Extraction of a Node from Availability List

We show in the following code how to obtain a new node from the availability list.

```
C
C       TO OBTAIN A NODE FOR LIST, FIRST CHECK IF AN
C       EMPTY NODE IS AVAILABLE OTHERWISE GIVE AN
C       ERROR MESSAGE
C
            IF (AVAIL.EQ.O) CALL ERROR
            NEWNOD = AVAIL
C       NOW WE HAVE THE NODE, ADVANCE THE AVAIL POINTER
            AVAIL = LINK (AVAIL)
                .
                .
                .
```

Figure 5.9(a) shows extraction of a node from the availability list. The node extracted becomes part of the list which would be used to display a graphic structure. NEWNOD gives us the pointer to the node just extracted from the availability list and AVAIL pointer is modified to give the top of the availability list. If the list is exhausted, this could be checked by looking at the null link; the error message should be printed out, indicating that the list is exhausted.

5.4.2 Addition of a Node to Availability List

We show a code to return a node to the availability list. Again, we note that the declaration statements are missing.

```
C
C       TO RETURN A NODE TO THE AVAILABILITY LIST
C
            LINK (OLDNOD) = AVAIL
            AVAIL = OLDNOD
                .
                .
                .
```

When the node is being returned to the availability list, we must update the pointers and links.

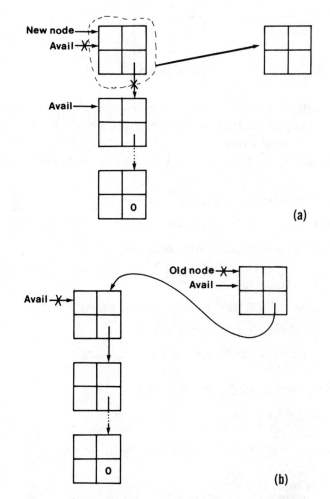

Figure 5.9 (a) Extraction of a node from availability
list. **(b)** Addition of a node to availability
list

5.4.3 Node Construction Routines

Let us construct nodes for a graphic problem. A typical node
contains four fields.

We will write an integer function called CNS which will accept as arguments the four values to be assigned to the fields of the new node. The value returned by function CNS will represent a pointer to the newly created node.

```
C
C       CONSTRUCTOR ROUTINE FOR NODES
C
        INTEGER FUNCTION CNS (CHART,XA,YB,NLINK)
C
C       THE LIST STRUCTURE DECLARATION
C
        COMMON X(1000), Y(1000), CHAR(1000), LINK(1000), AVAIL
        INTEGER CHAR,AVAIL,CNS,CHART
C
C       CHECK WHETHER AVAIL LIST IS EMPTY
C
            IF (AVAIL.GT.0) GO TO 10
C
            PRINT*, "INSUFFICIENT STORAGE"
            STOP
C
C       PICK OFF A NODE TO BE USED
C
10          CNS = AVAIL
            AVAIL = LINK (AVAIL)
C
C       FILL IN THE FIELDS FOR THE NEW NODE
C
            X(CNS) = XA
            Y(CNS) = YB
            CHAR(CNS) = CHART
            LINK(CNS) = NLINK
C
            RETURN
            END
```

Suppose we have to generate the following points:

$$LINE = CNS\ (\text{"A"},0.,0.,0)$$
$$LINE = CNS\ (\text{"B"},1.,1.,LINE)$$
$$LINE = CNS\ (\text{"C"},2.,2.,LINE)$$

In this example, variable LINE represents a pointer to the resulting line, and the value of LINE is updated as a result of

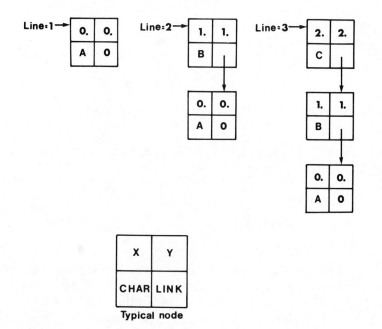

Figure 5.10 Line construction using function CNS

each call to function CNS after it is used as the link value of the node.

5.5 DATA-INDEPENDENT OPERATIONS OF LISTS

We distinguish between the operations on the data and the operations on their structure. The latter operation is the price one pays in order to organize data in a logical and manipulative form. Of course, one hopes that overall processing time will be better using data structure concepts than otherwise.

Some of the data-independent operations we need are:

(i) Pointers
(ii) Locating last node

(iii) Chaining two lists

(iv) Deletion of nodes

(v) Duplication of lists

5.5.1 Pointers

There are several types of pointers. All of these could be classified into two categories:

(i) External pointers

(ii) Internal pointers

(i) External Pointers ———

The external pointers are those pointers which are not fields of a node—for example, top pointers, pointing to the first node, or pointers which point to individual nodes.

It is noted that for a linearly linked list the top pointer is the only way we can enter the list. Therefore, all operations on the list must begin at the top of the list and by following the links, we proceed down the list. This, of course, is one of the deficiencies of the linearly linked list. Wastage of time is significant if we operate on the bottom portion of the list, yet we have to enter at the top in order to reach our position in the list. We can see that this difficulty does not occur in the array structure.

(ii) Internal Pointers ———

The internal pointers are those pointers which are actually fields of nodes—e.g., entries of vector LINK.

Implementation of a garbage collection scheme discussed later would involve incorporating some methods of distinguishing between internal and external pointers.

5.5.2 Locating Last Node

Sometimes it is useful to know the last node of a list. We will write a routine to do this.

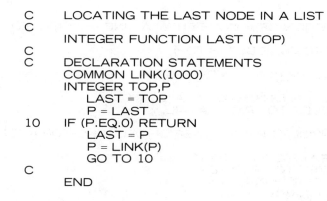

```
C       LOCATING THE LAST NODE IN A LIST
C
        INTEGER FUNCTION LAST (TOP)
C
C       DECLARATION STATEMENTS
        COMMON LINK(1000)
        INTEGER TOP,P
           LAST = TOP
           P = LAST
10      IF (P.EQ.0) RETURN
           LAST = P
           P = LINK(P)
           GO TO 10
C
        END
```

This function returns either 0 for no node in a list or returns the pointer to the last node.

5.5.3 Chaining Two Lists

We wish to chain two lists together so that the last node of the first list points to the first node of the second list.

```
C
C       CHAINING TWO LINEARLY LINKED LISTS
        INTEGER FUNCTION CHAIN (TOP1,TOP2)
C       DECLARATION STATEMENTS
        COMMON LINK(1000)
        INTEGER TOP1, TOP2
           LINK (LAST(TOP1)) = TOP2
           CHAIN = TOP1
           RETURN
        END
```

5.5.4 Deletion of Nodes

We should write a subroutine DLT which accepts two parameters:

P—A pointer identifying the node to be deleted.

TOP—TOP pointer designating the beginning of the list.

```
C
C       DELETION OF A NODE FROM A LINEARLY LINKED LIST
C
        SUBROUTINE DLT (P,TOP)
C
C       DECLARATION STATEMENTS
C
        COMMON LINK(1000), AVAIL
        INTEGER TOP,P,Q,R, AVAIL
C
C       CONSIDER SPECIAL CASE OF DELETING TOP NODE
C
        IF (P.NE.TOP) GO TO 10
C       MODIFY TOP POINTER
            TOP = LINK(TOP)
            LINK(P) = AVAIL
            AVAIL = P
        RETURN
C
C       SEARCH FOR THE PREDECESSOR OF P
C
10      Q = TOP
11      R = Q
        Q = LINK(Q)
C       IF Q IS ZERO THEN NODE IS NOT IN THE LIST
        IF (Q.EQ.0) CALL ERROR
        IF (Q.NE.P) GO TO 11
C       FOUND THE PREDECESSOR i.e. R
            LINK(R) = LINK(P)
C       RETURN THE NODE OF AVAILABILITY
            LINK(P) = AVAIL
            AVAIL = P
        RETURN
        END
```

5.5.5 Duplication of List

An integer function DUP is used to duplicate a list. The duplicated list will have a reverse order.

```
C       DUPLICATING LIST
        INTEGER FUNCTION DUP(TOP)
C       DECLARATION STATEMENTS
        COMMON LINK(1000)
        INTEGER P, DUP,TOP
            DUP = 0
            P = TOP
10      IF (P.EQ.0) RETURN
            DUP = CNS(DATA OF P,DUP)
            P = LINK(P)
            GO TO 10
        END
```

In situations where we wish to delete an entire list rather than just a single node, we need not invoke subroutine DLT. Instead, we use

AVAIL = CHAIN (AVAIL,TOP)

We should make sure that there are no pointers left which point to this list. Otherwise, some unpleasant results may occur.

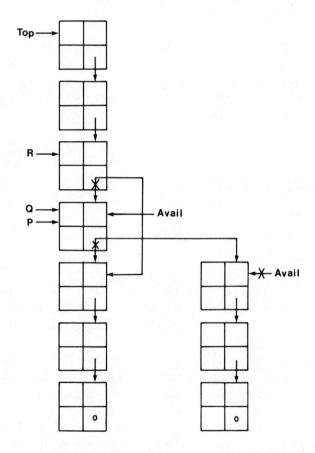

Figure 5.11 Deletion of a node and adding it to the availability list

We noted previously that it is a programmer's responsibility to return nodes to the availability list as soon as they are no longer needed.

There is a complementary technique used by actual list processing languages (LISP) called *garbage collection*. In this approach, when the construction function finds the availability list empty, it invokes the GBCR. GBCR scans through all the lists and returns to the availability list those nodes which are not pointed at by any pointer in the program. Consequently, the user is freed from the burden of having to liberate unused nodes. This scheme will be impractical to implement within the framework of our linearly linked list for the following reasons:

(i) Garbage collection procedure is a very time-consuming procedure.

(ii) In FORTRAN, we use integers as pointers, with the result that there is no way of determining which nodes are not pointed at by pointers external to the linked list.

5.6 APPLICATION TO COMPUTER GRAPHICS

One of the most exciting applications of list processing is the field of computer graphics, an area where we would like to create, manipulate, and output (i.e., draw) data structures representing graphic data.

From a computer point of view, the common aspect of different graphic structures is the fact that they can all be represented as a collection of points on the 2-D plane X-Y.

The kind of manipulation desired on graphic data can always be reduced to the basic operation of adding points to, and deleting points from, the description of the graphic structure.

5.6.1 Representation of Graphic Entity

A graphic entity can be represented by a linked list of nodes, each representing a single point on the X-Y plane. Therefore, each node will contain two data items, the X and Y coordinates of the point it represents. Since the linked list can be easily modified as far as adding and deleting of points are concerned, it is the best possible structure for graphic data.

Suppose we wish to generate a list to represent an intersection of two given lines (Fig. 5.12). This will require generation of two lists representing each line. The ideal solution will be to generate a list of predefined points. As a result, we have to define the smallest unit of distance which we can handle and spread the points along the line, one unit apart. The lists generated in this manner have a finite number of nodes and are shown in Fig. 5.12. Each node contains x and y coordinates of a point, a character identifying that point, and a link to the next node. Each line has its own list and a pointer to the top.

5.6.2 Graphic Processing Systems

It sometimes will be desirable to draw these two lines together. In that event, we will consider the two lists as primitive for creation of more elaborate graphic structures. We already know that to draw these two lines together we should merge these lists; hence, we should be able to merge line 1 and line 2 to form a cross. A shift operation is a "mixed-mode" operation, because in a shift, two operations may be necessary: first, merging and second, arithmetic operation shifting the intersection of the lines to a new point. Let us assume that the center of the cross is to be shifted by (10.0, 10.0). Since the center of the cross was at (2.0, 1.5), therefore all the points should be shifted by amount (8.0, 8.5). This shift is achieved by adding 8.0 to all the X coordinates and 8.5 to all the Y coordinates of the new list.

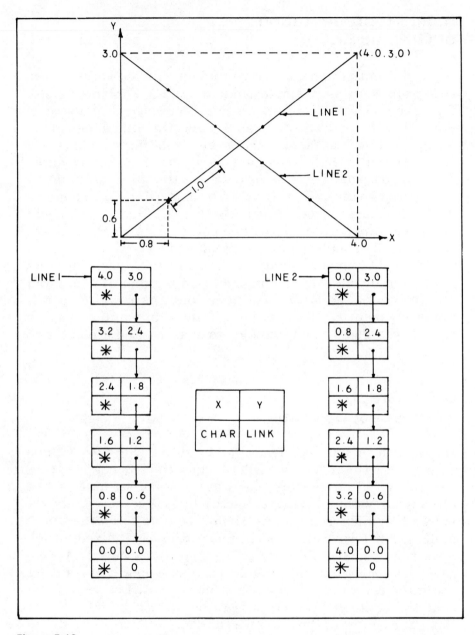

Figure 5.12

The above discussion leads to the conclusion that a graphic software system should have:

(i) Utility routines to operate on linked lists,

(ii) Primitive graphic items, such as lines, circles, etc.,

(iii) Manipulation routine to operate on primitive graphic items.

The details of the utility routines are described in Sections 5.4 and 5.5.

5.7 IMPLEMENTATION OF LINEAR LINKED LIST

In this implementation, we should use the line-printer as a graphic output device. This necessitates imposing the following conditions on our graphic representations:

(i) X-axis horizontal and Y-axis vertical—i.e., X-axis will be along the output page and Y along the rotation of paper.

(ii) We assume that a single line on the printer consists of 120 characters. Hence,

$$1 \leqslant X \geqslant 120$$

(iii) Our node should contain a character to be printed.

(iv) Since we can position the horizontal line only once, we should make sure that all values of Y are printed out. This will be achieved by sorting the Y values and for each line we will generate a buffer area of 120 characters.

5.8 CREATION OF PRIMITIVE GRAPHIC STRUCTURES

We will need a CNS routine to construct new nodes. Suppose we wish to create a list of four points with coordinates

$(X1,Y1)$, $(X2,Y2)$, $(X3,Y3)$, and $(X4,Y4)$, respectively. At each point, we want to print an asterisk.

```
C       CREATE A LINKED LIST TO REPRESENT
C       FOUR POINTS
        HEAD = CNS ('*',X1,Y1,0)
        HEAD = CNS ('*',X2,Y2,HEAD)
        HEAD = CNS ('*',X3,Y3,HEAD)
        HEAD = CNS ('*',X4,Y4,HEAD)
C       CREATE A DUMMY NODE
        HEAD = CNS ('*',1.,1.,HEAD)
```

Suppose we wish to add a node in a link list already formed. For example, the new point to be inserted might have coordinates (7.7,9.0) and we might wish to print the character "Z" at this point. Furthermore, the node representing this new point is to be inserted into the list following node P. We can accomplish that:

```
        LINK(P) = CNS ('Z',7.7,9.0,LINK(P))
```

Let us create a list to represent a line. Our primitive graphic structure:

```
C
C       CREATING A LIST TO REPRESENT A LINE
C
        INTEGER FUNCTION LINE (CHARL,X1,Y1,X2,Y2)
        COMMON X(1000), Y(1000), CHAR(1000), LINK(1000),AVAIL
        INTEGER CHAR, AVAIL, CNS, CHARL
C
            LINE = 0
            XD = X2 - X1
            YD = Y2 - Y1
C
C       CALCULATE THE RECIPROCAL DISTANCE BETWEEN THE TWO
C       END POINTS
C
            DS = 1./SQRT (XD**2 + YD**2)
C
C       NOW WE SHOULD CREATE 1/DS NODES IN THE LIST
C       LINES. INDEX SI WILL START WITH 0 AND WILL BE
C       INCREASED BY DS UNTIL IT REACHES 1.
C
            SI = 0.
10          LINE = CNS (CHAR, X1 + SI*XD, Y1 + SI*YD, LINE)
C           INCREMENT SI
            SI = SI + DS
            IF (SI.LE.1.) GO TO 10
```

```
C
C      ADD THE HEADER NODE
C
       LINE = CNS (' ', 1., 1., LINE)
       RETURN
C
       END
```

If we wish to create a line between (0.,0.) and (4.0,3.0) by printing crosses, we should call on the function LINE as follows:

$$\text{TOP} = \text{LINE ('+', 0., 0., 4.0, 3.0)}$$

This will create the link list to represent the line. Here TOP gives the pointer to the top of the list. A similar routine could be constructed for other primitive graphic structures such as CIRCLE, etc.

5.9 MANIPULATION OF GRAPHIC STRUCTURES

To this end, we need three routines in order to do mixed-mode operations.

SHIFT: This routine creates a shifted version of a graphic structure.

ROTATE: This function rotates a graphic entity around a particular point through a specified angle.

SCALE: This routine creates a magnified (or contracted) version of graph.

Coding of a FUNCTION ROTATE is shown on the following page. Details of the other two routines are given in Section 5.11.

```
           INTEGER FUNCTION ROTATE (TOP,CHARR,ALPHA,XC,YC)
C
C          THIS FUNCTION ROTATES A GRAPHIC PICTURE
C
           COMMON (X(1000), Y(1000), CHAR(1000), LINK(1000), AVAIL
           INTEGER TOP, P, AVAIL, CHAR, CNS, ROTATE, CHARR
           P = LINK(TOP)
           ROTATE = 0
C
C          TRANSFORM COORDINATES
C
10         XT = (X(P) - XC)* COS(ALPHA) - (Y(P) - YC)* SIN(ALPHA)
           YT = (XC - X(P))* SIN(ALPHA) + (Y(P) - YC)* COS(ALPHA)
           ROTATE =CNS(CHARR, (XC + XT), (YC + YT), ROTATE)
           P = LINK(P)
           IF (P.GT.0) GO TO 10
C
C          CREATE A DUMMY TOP NODE
C
           ROTATE = CNS(' ', 1., 1., ROTATE)
           RETURN
           END
```

5.10 GRAPHIC OUTPUT ROUTINES

We need two subroutines to output a graphic structure on a line printer. These are:

(i)   SORT subroutine
(ii) PRINT subroutine

A coding of these subroutines is shown in Section 5.11.

5.11 IMPLEMENTATION OF PROGRAM TO DRAW COMPLEX GRAPHIC STRUCTURES

On the pages that follow, a code written in FORTRAN language is provided to draw complex graphic structures. All the concepts of list processing discussed in the previous sections are implemented in the program. The program is tested on a Control Data Corporation Cyber 170 computer. However, with slight modifications, the program could be converted to any other computer. An example to draw a bicycle from the simple graphic structure—namely, line and circle—is given at the end. A standard printer was used to draw the bicycle.

The program is structured and extensively commented to be easily understood.

SUMMARY

In this chapter, several concepts of data structures relevant to computer graphics, such as static structures, dynamic structures, linearly linked lists, data-independent operations on lists, are explained. The data structure concepts are applied to develop graphic processing systems.

Finally, a FORTRAN program is given at the end of the chapter which draws a complicated graphic structure (a bicycle) from a primitive graphic structure (line and circle). A standard line printer was used to draw the bicycle. However, any other graphic display device may be used to display objects.

```
        PROGRAM BIKE(INPUT,OUTPUT)
C
C*******************************************************************
C*   THIS PROGRAM DRAWS A BIKE. IT USES LINEAR LINKED          *
C*   LIST TO STORE AND MANIPULATE DATA. ONLY TWO PRIMITIVE     *
C*   GRAPHIC STRUCTURES, LINE AND CIRCLE, ARE USED TO          *
C*   CONSTRUCT BIKE. VARIOUS SUBPROGRAMS ARE CALLED TO         *
C*   MANIPULATE DATA AND TO CONSTRUCT FINAL GRAPHIC DISPLAY    *
C*******************************************************************
C
C    DECLARE DATA TYPE AND COMMON DATA BLOCK
C
        CHARACTER CHAR(1000)
        COMMON /C1/X(1000),Y(1000),LINK(1000),AVAIL/C2/CHAR
        INTEGER SHIFTT,ROTATE,AVAIL,CROS1,CIRC1,CIRCLE,CIRC2
C
C    CREATE AVAILABILTY LIST AND INTIALIZE TOP POINTER
C
        DO 10 I = 1,999
          LINK(I) = I + 1
10      CONTINUE
        LINK(1000) = 0
        AVAIL = 1
C
C    CALL FUNCTION LINE TO CREATE PRIMITVE STRUCTURE OF A LINE.
C    ROTATE ABOVE LINE TO CONSTRUCT ANOTHER LINE AND THEN MERGE
C    IT WITH PREVIOUS LINE TO CONSTRUCT CROSS. THEN ROTATE CROSS
C    AND MERGE IT TO PRODUCE SPOKES OF A WHEEL.
C
        LINE1 = LINE('*',25.,15.,25.,35.)
        LINE2 = ROTATE(LINE1,'*',1.5707963,25.,25.)
        MER1 = MERGE(LINE1,LINE2)
        CROS1 = ROTATE(MER1,'*',0.7853982,25.,25.)
        MER2 = MERGE(MER1,CROS1)
C
C CONSTRUCT PRIMITIVE STRUCTURE OF A CIRCLE USING FUNCTION
C CIRCLE AND MERGE IT WITH CROSS TO PRODUCE A WHEEL.
C  SHIFT WHEEL1 AND MERGE IT TO CONSTRICT TWO WHEELS.
C
        CIRC1 = CIRCLE('*',25.,25.,10.)
        MER3 = MERGE(MER2,CIRC1)
        CIRC2 = CIRCLE('*',25.,25.,4.)
        MER4 = MERGE(MER3,CIRC2)
        IWH = SHIFTT(MER4,'*',40.,0.)
        MER5 = MERGE(MER4,IWH)
C
C    CONSTRUCT VARIOUS LINES FOR HORIZONTAL BAR, SEAT, AND
C    VERTICAL BAR; MERGE THEM ONE BY ONE TO PREVIOUS
C    STRUCTURE TO CONSTRUCT COMPLETE BIKE.
C
        LINE3 = LINE('=',40.,5.,50.,5.)
        MRE6 = MERGE(MER5,LINE3)
        LINE4 = LINE('I',45.,5.,45.,15.)
        MER7 = MERGE(MER6,LINE4)
        LINE5 = LINE('*',25.,15.,65.,15.)
        MER8 = MERGE(MER7,LINE5)
C
C    CALL SUBROUTINE PRINT TO PRINT BIKE ON A LINE PRINTER
C
        CALL PRINT(MER8,1.0,0.0,1.0,0.0)
        STOP
        END
```

```
      INTEGER FUNCTION LINE(CHARL,X1,Y1,X2,Y2)
C
C     CHARL IS THE CHARACTER TO BE PLACED IN ALL THE POINTS OF THE LINE.
C     X1,Y1 AND X2,Y2 ARE THE COORDINATES OF THE TWO END POINTS OF THE
C     LINE TO BE CREATED.
C
      CHARACTER CHARL,CHAR(1000)
      INTEGER CNS,AVAIL
      COMMON /C1/X(1000),Y(1000),LINK(1000),AVAIL/C2/CHAR
      LINE=0
      XD=X2-X1
      YD=Y2-Y1
C
C     CALCULATE THE DISTANCE BETWEEN THE TWO END POINTS.
C
      DS=1./SQRT((XD**2)+(YD**2))
C
C     CREATE 1/DS NODES IN THE LAST LINE. THE INDEX SI WILL START AT
C     0 AND WILL BE INCREMENTED BY DS UNTIL IT REACHES 1.0.
C
      SI=0.
      WHILE (SI .LE. 1.) DO
C
C     CREATE A NODE FOR THE LIST. THE X AND Y COORDINATES ARE CALCULATED
C     AS A FUNCTION OF SI USING THE LINEAR PROPERTIES OF THE LINE.
C
         LINE=CNS(CHARL,X1+SI*XD,Y1+SI*YD,LINE)
C
C     INCREMENT SI.
C
         SI=SI+DS
      END WHILE
C
C     ADD THE HEADER AND RETURN
C
      LINE=CNS(' ',1.,1.,LINE)
      RETURN
      END




      INTEGER FUNCTION CNS(CHART,XA,YA,NLINK)
C
C     THIS FUNCTION CONSTRUCTS THE NODES FOR THE LIST.
C
      CHARACTER CHART,CHAR(1000)
      COMMON /C1/X(1000),Y(1000),LINK(1000),AVAIL/C2/CHAR
      INTEGER AVAIL
C
C     CHECK WHETHER AVAIL IS EMPTY.
C
      IF(AVAIL .LE. 0) THEN
         PRINT *,' LIST IS EMPTY'
         RETURN
      END IF
C
C     PICK OFF A NODE TO BE USED
C
      CNS=AVAIL
C
C     TAKE THE NODE OFF THE LIST OF AVAILABLE STORAGE.
C
      AVAIL=LINK(AVAIL)
C
C     FILL IN THE FIELDS FOR THE NEW NODE.
C
      X(CNS)=XA
      Y(CNS)=YA
      CHAR(CNS)=CHART
      LINK(CNS)=NLINK
      RETURN
      END
```

```
      INTEGER FUNCTION CIRCLE(CHARL,XC,YC,RAD)
C
C     THIS FUNCTION PRODUCES A LIST WITH THE COORDINATES OF THE CIRCLE.
C
      CHARACTER CHAR(1000)
      COMMON /C1/X(1000),Y(1000),LINK(1000),AVAIL/C2/CHAR
      INTEGER CNS,AVAIL
      CIRCLE=0
      XA=RAD
      YA=0.
      DS=1./(2.*3.145927*RAD)
      DA=1./RAD
      SI=0.
      WHILE (SI .LE. 1.) DO
         YA=YA+(XA*DA)
         XA=XA-(YA*DA)
         CIRCLE=CNS(CHARL,XC+XA,YC+YA,CIRCLE)
         SI=SI+DS
      END WHILE
      CIRCLE=CNS(' ',1.,1.,CIRCLE)
      RETURN
      END




      INTEGER FUNCTION ROTATE(TOP,CHARR,ALPHA,XC,YC)
C
C     THIS FUNCTION ROTATES THE GRAPHIC ENTRY
C
      CHARACTER CHARR,CHAR(1000)
      COMMON /C1/X(1000),Y(1000),LINK(1000),AVAIL/C2/CHAR
      INTEGER TOP,P,CNS,AVAIL
      P=LINK(TOP)
      ROTATE=0
      WHILE (P .GT. 0) DO
         XXX=((X(P)-XC)*COS(ALPHA))+((Y(P)-YC)*SIN(ALPHA))
         YYY=((XC-X(P))*SIN(ALPHA))+((Y(P)-YC)*COS(ALPHA))
         ROTATE=CNS(CHARR,(XC+XXX),(YC+YYY),ROTATE)
         P=LINK(P)
      END WHILE
      ROTATE=CNS(' ',1.,1.,ROTATE)
      RETURN
      END




      INTEGER FUNCTION SHIFTT(TOP,CHARS,SX,SY)
C
C     THIS ROUTINE PERFORMS A SHIFT ON A GRAPHIC ENTRY.
C     CHARS IS THE CHARACTER TO BE USED FOR THE SHIFTED VERSION. SX AND
C     SY ARE THE QUANTITIES BY WHICH THE GRAPH IS TO BE SHIFTED.
C
      CHARACTER CHARS,CHAR(1000)
      COMMON /C1/X(1000),Y(1000),LINK(1000),AVAIL/C2/CHAR
      INTEGER TOP,P,CNS,AVAIL
C
C     P IS THE WANDERING POINTER WHICH WILL SCAN DOWN THE LIST. IT IS
C     INITIALIZED TO THE FIRST NODE FOLLOWING THE HEADER.
C
      P=LINK(TOP)
      SHIFTT=0
C
C     CREATE A NODE OF THE NEW LIST. THE NEW COORDINATES ARE CALCULATED
C     BY ADDING THE SHIFT VALUES TO THE COORDINATES IN THE LIST.
C
      WHILE (P .GT. 0) DO
         SHIFTT=CNS(CHARS,X(P)+SX,Y(P)+SY,SHIFTT)
C
C     ADVANCE THE POINTER P ALONG THE LINKS OF THE LIST.
C
         P=LINK(P)
      END WHILE
C
C     CREATE THE HEADER FOR THE NEW LIST AND RETURN
C
      SHIFTT=CNS(' ',1.,1.,SHIFTT)
      RETURN
      END
```

```
      INTEGER FUNCTION MERGE(TOP1,TOP2)
C
C     THIS FUNCTION MERGES TWO LISTS.
C     TOP1 AND TOP2 ARE POINTERS TO THE HEADERS OF THE TWO LISTS WHICH WE
C     WISH TO CONCATENATE. THE FUNCTION RETURNS AS ITS VALUE A POINTER TO
C     THE HEADER OF THE CONCATENATED LIST.
C
      CHARACTER CHAR(1000)
      COMMON /C1/X(1000),Y(1000),LINK(1000),AVAIL/C2/CHAR
      INTEGER TOP1,TOP2,AVAIL
C
C     ALTER THE LINK OF THE LAST NODE OF TOP1 TO POINT TO THE FIRST NODE
C     OF TOP2 FOLLOWING THE HEADER NODE.
C
      LINK(LAST(TOP1))=LINK(TOP2)
C
C     RETURN THE HEADER OF TOP2 TO AVAILABLE STORAGE.
C
      LINK(TOP2)=AVAIL
      AVAIL=TOP2
C
C     RETURN A POINTER TO THE HEADER OF TOP1. THIS HAS NOW BECOME THE
C     HEADER OF THE MERGED LIST.
C
      MERGE=TOP1
      RETURN
      END




      INTEGER FUNCTION LAST(TOP)
C
C     THIS FUNCTION FINDS THE LAST NODE OF A LIST
C
      CHARACTER CHAR(1000)
      COMMON /C1/X(1000),Y(1000),LINK(1000),AVAIL/C2/CHAR
      INTEGER TOP,P,AVAIL
      LAST=TOP
      P=LAST
      WHILE (P .NE. 0) DO
         LAST=P
         P=LINK(P)
      END WHILE
      RETURN
      END
```

```
      SUBROUTINE SORT(TOP)
C
C     THIS ROUTINE SORTS THE NODES ACCORDING TO THE Y COORDINATES.
C
      CHARACTER CHAR(1000)
      COMMON /C1/X(1000),Y(1000),LINK(1000),AVAIL/C2/CHAR
      INTEGER TOP,P,Q,R,AVAIL
C
C     TOP IS A POINTER TO THE HEADER OF THE LIST TO BE SORTED. P,Q AND
C     R ARE THE 3 POINTERS MOVING ALONG THE LIST.
C     CHECK FOR EMPTY LIST.
C
      IF(TOP .LT. 1) RETURN
      LATEST=0
      REPEAT
        LAST=LATEST
C
C     P POINTS TO THE FIRST OF 3 NODES UNDER EXAMINATION.
C
        P=TOP
C
C     AT THE START OF EACH SORTING PASS, INITIALIZE THE 3 POINTERS TO
C     THE TOP THREE NODES. CHECK EACH TIME WHETHER THE END POINTER HAS
C     REACHED THE TOP.
C
        Q=LINK(P)
        IF (Q .NE. LAST) THEN
          R=LINK(Q)
          IF (R .NE. LAST) THEN
            REPEAT
C
C     IF THE NODES Q AND R ARE IN ORDER, PROCEED TO COMPARE THE NEXT NODES.
C
              IF (Y(Q) .LT. Y(P)) THEN
C
C     THE FOLLOWING STATEMENTS PERFORM THE INTERCHANGE. MODIFY THE LINKS
C     ONLY TO REFLECT THE CHANGE.
C
                LATEST=Q
                LINK(P)=R
                LINK(Q)=LINK(R)
                LINK(R)=Q
              END IF
C
C     ADVANCE THE POINTER ALONG THE LINKS OF THE LIST.
C
              P=LINK(P)
              Q=LINK(P)
              R=LINK(Q)
C
C     IF THE LAST POINTER R HAS NOT YET REACHED THE END POINTER, LOOP
C     BACK TO RESUME THE SORTING PASS.
C
            UNTIL (R .EQ. LAST)
          END IF
        END IF
C
C     CHECK TO SEE IF ANOTHER PASS IS NECESSARY. RETURN TO PERFORM ANOTHER
C     PASS IF UNORDERED NODES HAVE BEEN FOUND.
C
      UNTIL (LATEST .EQ. LAST)
      RETURN
      END
```

```
       SUBROUTINE PRINT(TOP,SCAX,DISPX,SCAY,DISPY)
C
C   THIS SUBROUTINE PRINTS OUT A SET OF POINTS AS A PICTURE ON THE
C   PRINTER. TOP POINTS TO THE LIST OF POINTS.
C
       CHARACTER BUFFER(120),CHAR(1000)
       COMMON /C1/X(1000),Y(1000),LINK(1000),AVAIL/C2/CHAR
       INTEGER P,XC,YC,TOP,AVAIL
C
C   BUFFER IS A CHARACTER STRING OF LENGTH 120 THAT WILL STORE THE CHARACTERS.
C   SORT THE POINTS INTO PROPER ORDER.
C
       CALL SORT(TOP)
C
C   INITIALIZE P TO THE NODE FOLLOWING THE HEADER.
C
       P=LINK(TOP)
C
C   YC IS THE ROW NUMBER (Y COORDINATE) CURRENTLY BEING PRINTED.
C   THE MODIFIED VALUE OF Y IS ROUNDED TO AN INTEGER VARIABLE YC
C   THERFORE SEVERAL DIFFERENT Y'S CAN RESULT IN THE SAME YC.
C
       YC=(Y(P)*SCAY)+DISPY+0.5
C
C   NYC WILL CONTAIN THE ROW NUMBER OF THE NEXT ROW TO BE PRINTED.
C   IT IS INITIALIZED TO THE FIRST YC.
C
       NYC=YC
C
C   CLEAR THE BUFFER TO CONTAIN 120 BLANKS.
C
       REPEAT
           DO 10 I=1,120
               BUFFER(I)=' '
   10      CONTINUE
C
C   IF THE NEXT LINE TO BE PRINTED IS DIFFERENT FROM THE CURRENT LINE,
C   THEN PRINT OUT THE BLANK LINE.
C
           IF (YC .EQ. NYC) THEN
C
C   XC IS THE COORDINATE OF X IN THE BUFFER.
C
               REPEAT
                   XC=(X(P)*SCAX)+DISPX+.5
                   BUFFER(XC)=CHAR(P)
C
C   ADVANCE THE POINTER.
C
                   P=LINK(P)
C
C   IF THERE ARE NO MORE NODES IN THE LIST, THEN PRINT THE LAST
C   LINE AND TERMINATE THE SUBROUTINE CALL.
C
                   IF (P .GE. 1) THEN
C
C   DETERMINE THE NEXT Y COORDINATE TO BE PRINTED.
C
                       NYC=(Y(P)*SCAY)+DISPY+.5
C
C   COMPARE THE OLD COORDINATE WITH THE NEW ONE, IF THEY ARE EQUAL
C   CONTINUE TO ADD TO THE LINE. OTHERWISE PRINT OUT THE LINE.
C
               UNTIL (YC-NYC .NE. 0.)
                   END IF
           END IF
   30      PRINT 200, BUFFER
C
C   DECREMENT THE CURRENT Y COORDINATE. IF THE LAST NODE HAS NOT BEEN
C   REACHED YET, THEN CONTINUE TO CLEAR THE BUFFER.
C
       YC=YC-1.
C
C   STOP WHEN THE LAST NODE IS REACHED.
C
       UNTIL (P .LE. 0)
  200  FORMAT (120A1)
       RETURN
       END
```

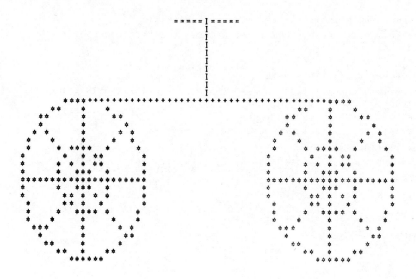

REFERENCES

Brillinger, P. C. and Cohen, D. J., *Introduction to Data Structures and Non Numeric Computations* (Englewood Cliffs, New Jersey: Prentice-Hall, 1972).

Lewis, T. G. and Smith, M. Z., *Applying Data Structures* (Boston, Massachusetts: Houghton Mifflin Company, 1976).

Mitchel, W. J., *Computer Aided Architectural Design* (New York: Petrocelli Charter, 1977).

6
TWO-DIMENSIONAL GRAPHICS

6.1 INTRODUCTION

A graphic system should allow the programmer to define pictures that include a variety of transformations. For example, a programmer should be able to magnify a picture for clarity or reduce it for more visibility. He or she should be able to rotate, translate, and combine all these operations. The ability to transform these points, lines, and characters is basic to computer graphics. All of these transformations can be accomplished using the mathematical techniques discussed in this and the next chapter.

6.2 TRANSFORMATION

As discussed in Chap. 4, a point can be represented by a position vector $[x, y]$. A line can be defined by two points. The position and orientation of the line joining these two points can be changed by operating on these two points. The transformation of a point or a line may consist of translation, rotation, and scaling.

6.2.1 Translation

A point or a line can be translated by rigidly moving it parallel or axially from one position to another. A translation of a line is shown in Fig. 6.1.

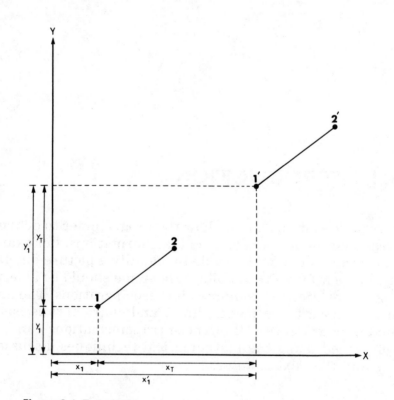

Figure 6.1 Translation

The form of the translation of a point is:

$$x_1^1 = x_1 + x_T$$

$$y_1^1 = y_1 + y_T$$

A similar formula will apply to the second point. This is achieved by changing the subscript 1 to 2.

6.2.2 Rotation

A point or a line can be rotated by rigidly rotating it from one position to another, as shown in Fig. 6.2.

To rotate a point clockwise through an angle θ about the origin of the coordinate system, we have:

$$x_1^1 = R \cos(\emptyset - \theta)$$

and

$$y_1^1 = R \sin(\emptyset - \theta)$$

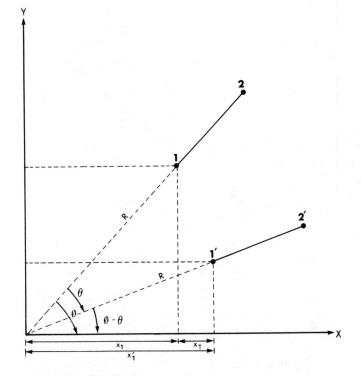

Figure 6.2 Rotation

Using the identities

$$\cos(\emptyset - \theta) = \cos\emptyset \cos\theta + \sin\emptyset \sin\theta$$
$$\sin(\emptyset - \theta) = \sin\emptyset \cos\theta - \sin\theta \cos\emptyset$$

and noting that

$$x_1 = R \cos\emptyset$$
$$y_1 = R \sin\emptyset$$

we have

$$x_1^1 = x_1 \cos\theta + y_1 \sin\theta$$

and

$$y_1^1 = -x_1 \sin\theta + y_1 \cos\theta$$

Changing the subscript 1 to 2 will give the formulas for the second point.

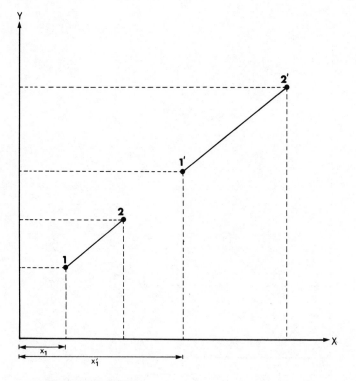

Figure 6.3 Scaling

6.2.3 Scaling

A position vector of a point or a line can be scaled by multiplying by a simple scalar number. The scaling operation is shown in Fig. 6.3.

The scaling transformations are:

$$x_1^1 = S\, x_1$$
$$y_1^1 = S\, y_1$$

Changing the subscript 1 to 2 will give the formulas for the second point.

6.3 MATRIX REPRESENTATION

Two-dimensional transformations of a point can be represented by matrix notation (see Appendix A for a brief discussion of matrix algebra) as follows:

Translation is given by

$$\begin{Bmatrix} x_1^1 \\ y_1^1 \end{Bmatrix} = \begin{bmatrix} 1 & 0 & x_T \\ 0 & 1 & y_T \end{bmatrix} \begin{Bmatrix} x_1 \\ y_1 \\ 1 \end{Bmatrix}$$

Rotation is given by

$$\begin{Bmatrix} x_1^1 \\ y_1^1 \end{Bmatrix} = \begin{bmatrix} \cos\theta & \sin\theta \\ \sin\theta & \cos\theta \end{bmatrix} \begin{Bmatrix} x_1 \\ y_1 \end{Bmatrix}$$

and scaling is giving by

$$\begin{Bmatrix} x_1^1 \\ y_1^1 \end{Bmatrix} = \begin{bmatrix} S & 0 \\ 0 & S \end{bmatrix} \begin{Bmatrix} x_1 \\ y_1 \end{Bmatrix}$$

The combination of all transformations into a single 2×2 matrix is not possible. This difficulty stems from the fact that translation requires a 2×3 matrix. We can overcome this difficulty by introducing the concept of homogeneous coordinates. Two-dimensional transformation can be represented in homogeneous coordinates by a 3×3 matrix.

6.4 HOMOGENEOUS COORDINATES

The homogeneous representation of an object in n dimensional space is an object in $(n + 1)$ dimensional space. The coordinates in n-space are called ordinary coordinates, and those in $(n + 1)$ space are called homogeneous coordinates. Two-dimensional data where the position of a point is given by the pair $[x \ y]$ in ordinary coordinates are represented by three homogeneous coordinates $[hx \ hy \ h]$. It should be noted that h is an arbitrary number and usually is taken as unity for ease of calculation.

6.5 TWO-DIMENSIONAL TRANSLATION AND HOMOGENEOUS COORDINATES

Within the framework of a general 2×2 matrix, it is not possible to combine translation, rotation, and scaling. This difficulty is overcome by introducing a third component to point vectors $[x \ y]$, making them $[x \ y \ 1]$, and the third column is added to the transformation matrices.

The parameters of the 3×3 transformation matrix can be arranged to make the matrix represent the simple transformations of translation, rotation, and scaling.

Translation:

$$\begin{Bmatrix} x^1 \\ y^1 \\ 1 \end{Bmatrix} = \begin{bmatrix} 1 & 0 & x_T \\ 0 & 1 & y_T \\ 0 & 0 & 1 \end{bmatrix} \begin{Bmatrix} x \\ y \\ 1 \end{Bmatrix} \qquad (6.1)$$

Rotation:

$$\begin{Bmatrix} x^1 \\ y^1 \\ 1 \end{Bmatrix} = \begin{bmatrix} \cos\theta & \sin\theta & 0 \\ -\sin\theta & \cos\theta & 0 \\ 0 & 0 & 1 \end{bmatrix} \begin{Bmatrix} x \\ y \\ 1 \end{Bmatrix} \qquad (6.2)$$

Scaling:

$$\begin{Bmatrix} x^1 \\ y^1 \\ 1 \end{Bmatrix} = \begin{bmatrix} S & 0 & 0 \\ 0 & S & 0 \\ 0 & 0 & 1 \end{bmatrix} \begin{Bmatrix} x \\ y \\ 1 \end{Bmatrix} \tag{6.3}$$

We will define scaling matrix by S, translation matrix by T and rotation matrix by R. The general transformation matrix M is

$$\begin{Bmatrix} x^1 \\ y^1 \\ 1 \end{Bmatrix} = M \begin{Bmatrix} x \\ y \\ 1 \end{Bmatrix} \tag{6.4}$$

where

$$M = STRT$$

6.6 TWO-DIMENSIONAL ROTATION ABOUT AN ARBITRARY AXIS

The rotation matrix defined by equation (6.2) allows points, lines, and objects to rotate about the origin. However, it is possible to transform an object about an arbitrary point. This is achieved by first translating the center of rotation to the origin, performing the required rotation, and then translating the result back to the original center of rotation.

To give an example, consider the triangle shown in Fig. 6.4(a). The coordinates of the vertices of the triangle must be expressed in homogeneous coordinates. These coordinates are given as column vectors of the matrix C for vertices 1, 2, and 3, respectively.

$$C = \begin{bmatrix} 3 & 1 & 3 \\ 3 & 3 & 1 \\ 1 & 1 & 1 \end{bmatrix}$$

The triangle is rotated by 90° about the axis passing through point 4 whose coordinates are [2 2 1] in homogeneous coordinates. Figure 6.4 shows these transformations. The final co-

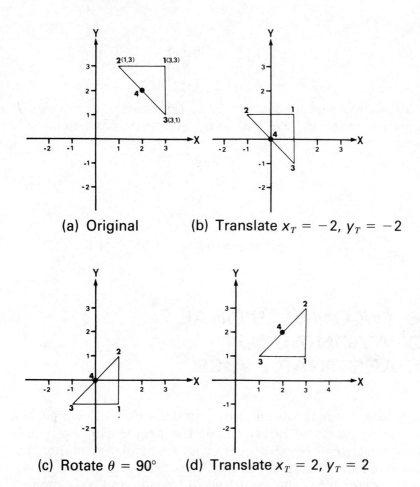

(a) Original   (b) Translate $x_T = -2$, $y_T = -2$

(c) Rotate $\theta = 90°$ (d) Translate $x_T = 2$, $y_T = 2$

Figure 6.4 Rotation about an arbitrary point

ordinates of the triangle are:

$$C^1 = \begin{bmatrix} 3 & 3 & 1 \\ 1 & 3 & 1 \\ 1 & 1 & 1 \end{bmatrix}$$

Mathematically, these transformations will require simple multiplication of four matrices to get the transformation matrix:

$$M = \begin{bmatrix} 1 & 0 & 0 \\ 0 & 1 & 0 \\ 0 & 0 & 1 \end{bmatrix}\begin{bmatrix} 1 & 0 & 2 \\ 0 & 1 & 2 \\ 0 & 0 & 1 \end{bmatrix}\begin{bmatrix} 0 & 1 & 0 \\ -1 & 0 & 0 \\ 0 & 0 & 1 \end{bmatrix}\begin{bmatrix} 1 & 0 & -2 \\ 0 & 1 & -2 \\ 0 & 0 & 1 \end{bmatrix}$$

$$M = \begin{bmatrix} 0 & 1 & 0 \\ -1 & 0 & 4 \\ 0 & 0 & 1 \end{bmatrix}$$

We note that the scaling matrix is an identity matrix. This means that the size of the triangle will not be altered. By applying the transformation matrix to the original coordinates, we get the final coordinates of the transformed triangle.

$$C' = MC$$

$$C' = \begin{bmatrix} 0 & 1 & 0 \\ -1 & 0 & 4 \\ 0 & 0 & 1 \end{bmatrix} \begin{bmatrix} 3 & 1 & 3 \\ 3 & 3 & 1 \\ 1 & 1 & 1 \end{bmatrix}$$

$$C' = \begin{bmatrix} 3 & 3 & 1 \\ 1 & 3 & 1 \\ 1 & 1 & 1 \end{bmatrix}$$

There is an important point to be noted here. Had the applied scaling matrix not been an identity matrix, then after the second translation shrinking or expanding would have occurred proportional to the sides of the triangle. Hence, the scaled triangle would either be inside or outside the triangle shown in Fig. 6.4(d), and be similarly oriented.

6.7 COMPUTER PROGRAM FOR TWO-DIMENSIONAL TRANSFORMATION

As an example, we show a computer code to:

(a) Rotate face shown in Fig. 6.5(a) by 360° in steps of 45° around origin.

(b) Rotate face around an arbitrary point one unit to the right of the back and one unit below the flat head as shown in Fig. 6.5(b). Use scaling factor S linearly related to θ. We are given that when $\theta = 0°$, $S = 1$ and when $\theta = 360°$, $S = 0$.

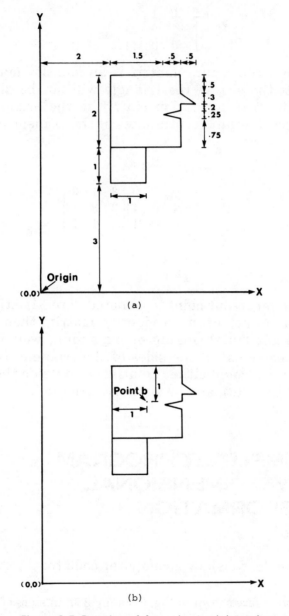

(a)

(b)

Figure 6.5 Rotation of face about origin and an arbitrary point b

The output from the program is shown in Figs. 6.6 and 6.7. The program calls on a series of subprograms from the computer library called the PLOT 10 library. The program and PLOT 10 subprograms are both written in FORTRAN language and were implemented on the Control Data Corporation Cyber 170 computer.

The program is structured and extensively commented to be easily understood.

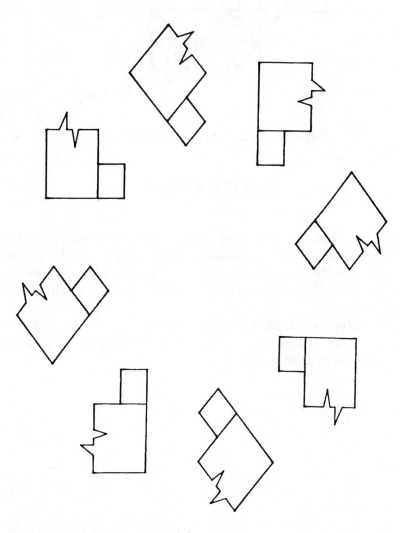

Figure 6.6 Rotation about origin

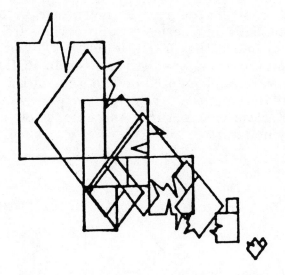

Figure 6.7 Rotation about an arbitrary point b

SUMMARY

In this chapter, several concepts relevant to two-dimensional graphics, such as homogeneous coordinates and 2-D transformation, are developed. The description of these is elementary, and is inclined toward vector graphics rather than raster graphics.

Finally, a FORTRAN program is given at the end of the chapter that employs the concepts developed in the two-dimensional graphics chapter.

```
       PROGRAM TRANFOR(DATA2,OUTPUT,INPUT=DATA2)
*************************************************************
*    THIS ROUTINE PERFORMS TRANSFORMATION ON A 2-D OBJECT   *
*************************************************************
       REAL SCALE(3,3),TRANS1(3,3),ROTATE(3,3),TRANS2(3,3),M(3,3)
      * ,INDATA(3,50),OUTDATA(3,50),TEMP1(3,3),TEMP2(3,3)
*************************************************************
*    READ IN DATA POINTS FOR THE FIGURE                     *
*************************************************************
       READ *,N,((INDATA(I,J),I=1,3),J=1,N)
       CALL INITT(30)
       CALL VWINDO(-7.5,15.,-7.5,15.)
       DO 20 L=1,2
       DO 10 I=45,405,45
         J=I-45
         THETA=(FLOAT(J)*3.141592654)/180.0
         IF (L.EQ.1) THEN
           CALL SCALEM (1.,SCALE)
           CALL TRANSM (0.,0.,TRANS1)
           CALL TRANSM (0.,0.,TRANS2)
           CALL ROTATEM (THETA,ROTATE)
         ELSE
           S=1.0-(1./360.)*J
           CALL SCALEM (S,SCALE)
           CALL TRANSM (3.,5.,TRANS1)
           CALL TRANSM (-3.5,-5.,TRANS2)
           CALL ROTATEM (THETA,ROTATE)
         END IF
*************************************************************
*    MULTIPLY THE MATRIXES TO GET THE TRANSFORMATION MATRIX M  *
*************************************************************
         CALL MATMUL(3,3,ROTATE,TRANS2,TEMP1)
         CALL MATMUL(3,3,TRANS1,TEMP1,TEMP2)
         CALL MATMUL(3,3,SCALE,TEMP2,M)
*************************************************************
*    USE MATRIX M TO GET THE TRANSFORMED MATRIX OUTDATA      *
*************************************************************
         CALL MATMUL(50,N,M,INDATA,OUTDATA)
*************************************************************
*    PLOT THE FIGURE                                        *
*************************************************************
         CALL PLOT(OUTDATA,N)
  10   CONTINUE
       CALL TINPUT(K)
       CALL NEWPAG
  20   CONTINUE
       CALL FINITT(0,767)
       STOP
       END
```

```
      SUBROUTINE ROTATEM (THETA,ROTATE)
*******************************************************************
*    THIS ROUTINE PRODUCES THE ROTATION MATRIX                   *
*******************************************************************
      REAL ROTATE (3,3)
      DO 10 I=1,3
      DO 10 J=1,3
        ROTATE(I,J)=0.0
 10   CONTINUE
      ROTATE(1,1)=COS(THETA)
      ROTATE(1,2)=SIN(THETA)
      ROTATE(2,1)=-SIN(THETA)
      ROTATE(2,2)=COS(THETA)
      ROTATE(3,3)=1.0
      RETURN
      END


      SUBROUTINE SCALEM(S,SCALE)
*******************************************************************
*    THIS ROUTINE PRODUCES THE SCALE MATRIX                      *
*******************************************************************
      REAL SCALE (3,3)
      DO 10 I=1,3
      DO 10 J=1,3
        SCALE(I,J)=0.0
        IF (I.EQ.J) SCALE(I,J)=S
 10   CONTINUE
      SCALE(3,3)=1.0
      RETURN
      END



      SUBROUTINE TRANSM (X,Y,TRANS)
*******************************************************************
*    THIS ROUTINE PRODUCES THE TRANSLATION MATRIXES              *
*******************************************************************
      REAL TRANS(3,3)
      DO 10 I=1,3
      DO 10 J=1,3
        TRANS(I,J)=0.0
        IF (I.EQ.J) TRANS(I,J)=1.0
 10   CONTINUE
      TRANS(1,3)=X
      TRANS(2,3)=Y
      RETURN
      END
```

```
        SURROUTINE MATMUL(MAX,N,A,B,C)
****************************************************************
*    THIS ROUTINE PERFORMS THE MATRIX MULTIPLICATION          *
****************************************************************
        REAL A(3,3),B(3,MAX),C(3,MAX)
        DO 1 I=1,3
          DO 1 J=1,N
            C(I,J)=0.0
            DO 1 K=1,3
              C(I,J)=C(I,J)+A(I,K)*B(K,J)
  1     CONTINUE
        RETURN
        END


        SURROUTINE PLOT(OUTDATA,N)
****************************************************************
*    THIS ROUTINE PLOTS OUT THE TRANSFORMED FIGURE            *
****************************************************************
        REAL OUTDATA(3,N)
        CALL MOVEA(OUTDATA(1,1),OUTDATA(2,1))
        DO 10 I=1,N
          CALL DRAWA(OUTDATA(1,I),OUTDATA(2,I))
  10    CONTINUE
        RETURN
        END
```

```
        15
        2.   4.  1.
        2.   3.  1.
        3.   3.  1.
        3.   4.  1.
        2.   4.  1.
        2.   6.  1.
        4.   6.  1.
        4.   5.5 1.
        4.5  5.2 1.
        4.   5.2 1.
        4.   5.  1.
        3.5  4.875 1.
        4.   4.75 1.
        4.   4.  1.
        3.   4.  1.
```

Data File

REFERENCES

Forrest, A. R., "Co-ordinates, Transformations and Visualization Techniques," CAD Group, Document No. 23, Cambridge University, Cambridge, England, June 1969.

Newmann, W. M. and Sproull, R. F., *Principles of Interactive Computer Graphics* (New York: McGraw-Hill Book Company, 1979).

Roberts, L. G., "Homogeneous Matrix Representation and Manipulation of N-Dimensional Constructs," Document MS 1405, Lincoln Laboratory, MIT, Cambridge, Massachusetts, May 1965.

Rogers, D. F. and Adams, A. J., *Mathematical Elements for Computer Graphics* (New York: McGraw-Hill Book Company, 1976).

7
THREE-DIMENSIONAL GRAPHICS

7.1 INTRODUCTION

Producing a realistic picture of a three-dimensional object on a two-dimensional display presents many problems. How is depth, the third dimension, to be displayed on the screen or plotter? How are parts of objects to be identified and removed from the picture? How are these objects rotated, translated, and scaled? A number of techniques have been developed to address these questions; the following sections describe these techniques.

7.1.1 Three-Dimensional Transformation

The representation and transformation of objects in three dimensions are usually performed in a Cartesian coordinate system. The three Cartesian coordinates $[x\ y\ z]$ are sufficient to represent a point in three dimensions.

A transformation such as rotation or scaling is represented by a 3×3 matrix. Multiplication of the position vector by this matrix yields a transformed position vector. Certain points (notably points at infinity) and certain transformations (notably translations and perspective projections) cannot be represented in this scheme. For these, we must expand the "homogeneous coordinates" concept from our previous two-dimensional analysis, described in Chap. 6, to three dimensions. We start by asserting that a point in a space $[x\ y\ z]$ is represented by a four-dimensional position vector $[x\ y\ z\ 1]$. The transformation of a point is given by:

$$\begin{Bmatrix} x^1 \\ y^1 \\ z^1 \\ 1 \end{Bmatrix} = M \begin{Bmatrix} x \\ y \\ z \\ 1 \end{Bmatrix} \tag{7.1}$$

where M is a transformation matrix.

The generalized 4×4 transformation matrix for three-dimensional homogeneous coordinates is:

$$M = \begin{bmatrix} a_{11} & a_{12} & a_{13} & a_{14} \\ a_{21} & a_{22} & a_{23} & a_{24} \\ a_{31} & a_{32} & a_{33} & a_{34} \\ a_{41} & a_{42} & a_{43} & a_{44} \end{bmatrix} \tag{7.2}$$

In a concise form, the transformation matrix is:

$$M = ST_f RT_i \tag{7.3}$$

where

T_i = initial translation matrix

R = rotation matrix

T_f = final translation matrix

S = scaling matrix

We note that for scaling and rotation we only need a 3×3 transformation matrix. But to generalize this matrix so as to include translation we need to add an extra row and column, thereby making it into a 4×4 generalized transformation matrix.

7.1.2 Three-Dimensional Scaling

The diagonal terms of the general 4×4 transformation produce local and overall scaling. For example:

$$\begin{Bmatrix} x^1 \\ y^1 \\ z^1 \\ 1 \end{Bmatrix} = \begin{bmatrix} a_{11} & 0 & 0 & 0 \\ 0 & a_{22} & 0 & 0 \\ 0 & 0 & a_{33} & 0 \\ 0 & 0 & 0 & 1 \end{bmatrix} \begin{Bmatrix} x \\ y \\ z \\ 1 \end{Bmatrix} = \begin{Bmatrix} a_{11}x \\ a_{22}y \\ a_{33}z \\ 1 \end{Bmatrix} \quad (7.4)$$

This shows the local scaling effect. Figure 7.1 shows a parallelopiped rescaled as a unit cube. Overall scaling is obtained by using the same local scaling in all three dimensions—i.e., $a_{11} = a_{22} = a_{33} = s$. Figure 7.2 shows a unit cube scaled to twice its size in linear dimensions.

$$\begin{Bmatrix} x^1 \\ y^1 \\ z^1 \\ 1 \end{Bmatrix} = \begin{bmatrix} s & 0 & 0 & 0 \\ 0 & s & 0 & 0 \\ 0 & 0 & s & 0 \\ 0 & 0 & 0 & 1 \end{bmatrix} \begin{Bmatrix} x \\ y \\ z \\ 1 \end{Bmatrix} = \begin{Bmatrix} sx \\ sy \\ sz \\ 1 \end{Bmatrix} \quad (7.5)$$

7.1.3 Three-Dimensional Shearing

The off-diagonal terms in the upper left 3×3 component matrix of the generalized 4×4 transformation matrix produce shearing in three dimensions—e.g.,

$$\begin{Bmatrix} x^1 \\ y^1 \\ z^1 \\ 1 \end{Bmatrix} = \begin{bmatrix} 1 & b & c & 0 \\ d & 1 & f & 0 \\ h & k & 1 & 0 \\ 0 & 0 & 0 & 1 \end{bmatrix} \begin{Bmatrix} x \\ y \\ z \\ 1 \end{Bmatrix} = \begin{Bmatrix} x + yd + hz \\ bx + y + kz \\ cx + fy + z \\ 1 \end{Bmatrix} \quad (7.6)$$

A simple three-dimensional shearing on a unit cube is shown in Fig. 7.3.

7.1.4 Three-Dimensional Rotations

In the previous sections, we saw that a 3×3 component matrix produced a combination of scaling and shearing. A rota-

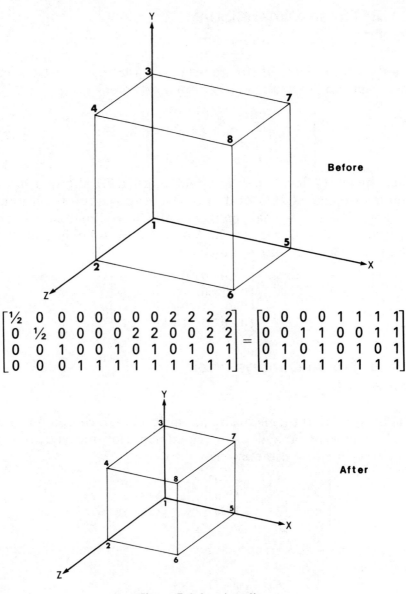

Figure 7.1 Local scaling

tion is defined by three separate matrices, one for each axis. These matrices are referred to as pitch, yaw, and roll. The pitch, yaw, and roll represent arbitrary rotations about the x, y, and z axes, respectively, as shown in Fig. 7.4.

The rotations are assumed to be positive in a right-hand

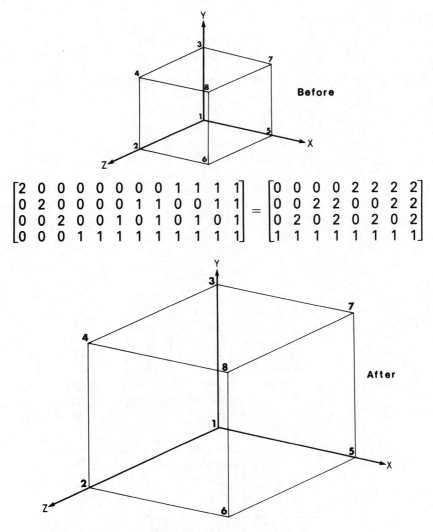

$$\begin{bmatrix} 2 & 0 & 0 & 0 & 0 & 0 & 0 & 0 & 1 & 1 & 1 & 1 \\ 0 & 2 & 0 & 0 & 0 & 0 & 1 & 1 & 0 & 0 & 1 & 1 \\ 0 & 0 & 2 & 0 & 0 & 1 & 0 & 1 & 0 & 1 & 0 & 1 \\ 0 & 0 & 0 & 1 & 1 & 1 & 1 & 1 & 1 & 1 & 1 & 1 \end{bmatrix} = \begin{bmatrix} 0 & 0 & 0 & 0 & 2 & 2 & 2 & 2 \\ 0 & 0 & 2 & 2 & 0 & 0 & 2 & 2 \\ 0 & 2 & 0 & 2 & 0 & 2 & 0 & 2 \\ 1 & 1 & 1 & 1 & 1 & 1 & 1 & 1 \end{bmatrix}$$

Figure 7.2 Overall scaling

sense as one looks from the origin outward along the axis of rotation.

For a rotation through an angle ψ about the z-axis as shown in Fig. 7.5, zeros appear in the third row and column, except for unity on the diagonal term. We have

$$x' = x \cos\psi + y \sin\psi$$
$$y' = -x \sin\psi + y \cos\psi$$

or

$$\begin{Bmatrix} x' \\ y' \end{Bmatrix} = \begin{bmatrix} \cos\psi & \sin\psi \\ -\sin\psi & \cos\psi \end{bmatrix} \begin{Bmatrix} x \\ y \end{Bmatrix} \tag{7.7}$$

Expanding to three dimensions and noting that z-dimensions

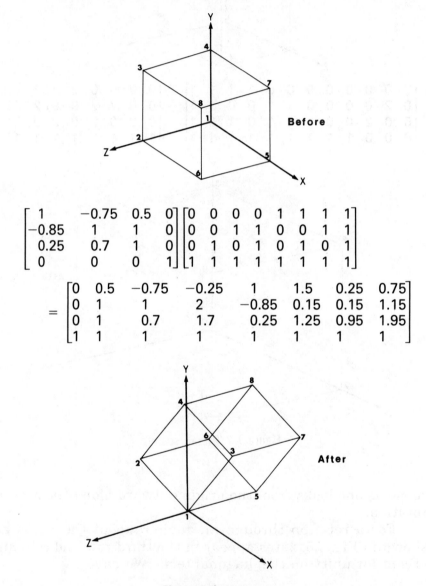

$$\begin{bmatrix} 1 & -0.75 & 0.5 & 0 \\ -0.85 & 1 & 1 & 0 \\ 0.25 & 0.7 & 1 & 0 \\ 0 & 0 & 0 & 1 \end{bmatrix} \begin{bmatrix} 0 & 0 & 0 & 0 & 1 & 1 & 1 & 1 \\ 0 & 0 & 1 & 1 & 0 & 0 & 1 & 1 \\ 0 & 1 & 0 & 1 & 0 & 1 & 0 & 1 \\ 1 & 1 & 1 & 1 & 1 & 1 & 1 & 1 \end{bmatrix}$$

$$= \begin{bmatrix} 0 & 0.5 & -0.75 & -0.25 & 1 & 1.5 & 0.25 & 0.75 \\ 0 & 1 & 1 & 2 & -0.85 & 0.15 & 0.15 & 1.15 \\ 0 & 1 & 0.7 & 1.7 & 0.25 & 1.25 & 0.95 & 1.95 \\ 1 & 1 & 1 & 1 & 1 & 1 & 1 & 1 \end{bmatrix}$$

Figure 7.3 Shearing

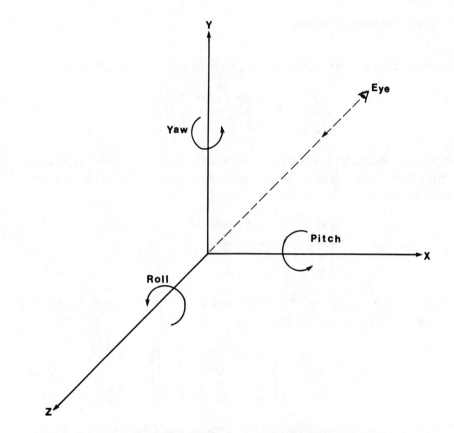

Figure 7.4 Pitch, yaw, and roll rotations

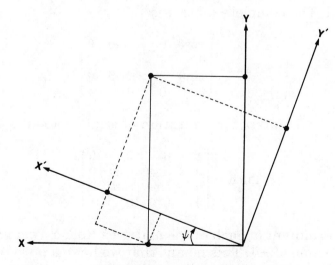
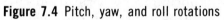

Figure 7.5 Roll rotation ψ z-axis

do not change, we have a three-dimensional matrix as

$$\begin{Bmatrix} x' \\ y' \\ z' \end{Bmatrix} = \begin{bmatrix} \cos\psi & \sin\psi & 0 \\ -\sin\psi & \cos\psi & 0 \\ 0 & 0 & 1 \end{bmatrix} \begin{Bmatrix} x \\ y \\ z \end{Bmatrix} \tag{7.8}$$

We now construct a four-dimensional generalized matrix roll from the three-dimensional rotation matrix by adding a row and a column.

$$\begin{Bmatrix} x' \\ y' \\ z \\ 1 \end{Bmatrix} = \begin{bmatrix} \cos\psi & \sin\psi & 0 & 0 \\ -\sin\psi & \cos\psi & 0 & 0 \\ 0 & 0 & 1 & 0 \\ 0 & 0 & 0 & 1 \end{bmatrix} \begin{Bmatrix} x \\ y \\ z \\ 1 \end{Bmatrix} \tag{7.9}$$

The 4×4 matrix relating primed and unprimed coordinates shown above is called the roll.

$$\text{Roll} = \begin{bmatrix} \cos\psi & \sin\psi & 0 & 0 \\ -\sin\psi & \cos\psi & 0 & 0 \\ 0 & 0 & 1 & 0 \\ 0 & 0 & 0 & 1 \end{bmatrix} \tag{7.10}$$

Similarly, yaw is obtained by a rotation through an angle $\emptyset$ about the y-axis. Zeros appear in the second row and the second column of the yaw matrix, except for unity on the main diagonal. The complete matrix is

$$\text{Yaw} = \begin{bmatrix} \cos\emptyset & 0 & -\sin\emptyset & 0 \\ 0 & 1 & 0 & 0 \\ \sin\emptyset & 0 & \cos\emptyset & 0 \\ 0 & 0 & 0 & 1 \end{bmatrix} \tag{7.11}$$

The rotation matrix for a rotation of angle θ about x-axis is

$$\text{Pitch} = \begin{bmatrix} 1 & 0 & 0 & 0 \\ 0 & \cos\theta & \sin\theta & 0 \\ 0 & -\sin\theta & \cos\theta & 0 \\ 0 & 0 & 0 & 1 \end{bmatrix} \tag{7.12}$$

The determinant of each of the matrices Roll, Yaw, and Pitch has the value of $+1$. This means that we have a pure rotation about the origin in a positive direction as defined by the right-hand rule.

7.1.5 Three-Dimensional Translation

A point in space could be translated by giving it a movement of $(x_t y_t z_t)$ in the x, y, and z directions, respectively. Therefore, the coordinates of a point translated from the P to P' position are given by

$$x' = x + x_t$$
$$y' = y + y_t$$
$$z' = z + z_t$$

These equations in matrix notation are conveniently expressed as

$$
\begin{Bmatrix} x' \\ y' \\ z' \\ 1 \end{Bmatrix} = \begin{bmatrix} 1 & 0 & 0 & x_t \\ 0 & 1 & 0 & y_t \\ 0 & 0 & 1 & z_t \\ 0 & 0 & 0 & 1 \end{bmatrix} \begin{Bmatrix} x \\ y \\ z \\ 1 \end{Bmatrix}
\tag{7.13}
$$

This matrix, relating primed coordinates to unprimed coordinates, is called the translation matrix.

7.1.6 Rotation about an Arbitrary Point

The rotation about an arbitrary point requires three operations. These are:

(i) Translation of an object to origin.

(ii) Rotation of an object.

(iii) Translation of an object to a desired point.

Thus, the matrix which will achieve all these transformations is given by

$$M = ST_f R T_i$$

where

S = Scaling matrix

T_f = Final translation matrix

R = Rotation matrix formed by multiplying roll, yaw, and pitch

T = Initial translation matrix

These matrices are

$$S = \begin{bmatrix} s & 0 & 0 & 0 \\ 0 & s & 0 & 0 \\ 0 & 0 & s & 0 \\ 0 & 0 & 0 & 1 \end{bmatrix}$$

$$T_f = \begin{bmatrix} 1 & 0 & 0 & x_f \\ 0 & 1 & 0 & y_f \\ 0 & 0 & 1 & z_f \\ 0 & 0 & 0 & 1 \end{bmatrix}$$

$$R = \text{Roll} \times \text{Yaw} \times \text{Pitch} = \begin{bmatrix} a_{11} & a_{12} & a_{13} & 0 \\ a_{21} & a_{22} & a_{23} & 0 \\ a_{31} & a_{32} & a_{33} & 0 \\ 0 & 0 & 0 & 1 \end{bmatrix}$$

$$T_i = \begin{bmatrix} 1 & 0 & 0 & -x_i \\ 0 & 1 & 0 & -y_i \\ 0 & 0 & 1 & -z_i \\ 0 & 0 & 0 & 1 \end{bmatrix}$$

On the multiplication of these matrices, we find that the transformation matrix is

$$M = \begin{bmatrix} sa_{11} & sa_{12} & sa_{13} & -s(a_{11}x_i + a_{12}y_i + a_{13}z_i) + sx_f \\ sa_{21} & sa_{22} & sa_{23} & -s(a_{21}x_i + a_{22}y_i + a_{23}z_i) + sy_f \\ sa_{31} & sa_{32} & sa_{33} & -s(a_{31}x_i + a_{32}y_i + a_{33}z_i) + sz_f \\ 0 & 0 & 0 & 1 \end{bmatrix} \quad (7.14)$$

It should be noted that rotations are calculated by matrix multiplication and that, in consequence, three-dimensional rotations are noncommutative; in other words, the order of application of the rotations will affect the final result. To show this, consider a rotation about the x-axis followed by an equal rotation about the y-axis—i.e., $\theta = \emptyset$, using equations (7.11) and (7.12).

$$R = \begin{bmatrix} 1 & 0 & 0 & 0 \\ 0 & \cos\theta & \sin\theta & 0 \\ 0 & -\sin\theta & \cos\theta & 0 \\ 0 & 0 & 0 & 1 \end{bmatrix} \begin{bmatrix} \cos\emptyset & 0 & -\sin\emptyset & 0 \\ 0 & 1 & 0 & 0 \\ \sin\emptyset & 0 & \cos\emptyset & 0 \\ 0 & 0 & 0 & 1 \end{bmatrix}$$

$$= \begin{bmatrix} \cos\theta & 0 & -\sin\theta & 0 \\ \sin^2\theta & \cos\theta & \cos\theta\sin\theta & 0 \\ \cos\theta\sin\theta & -\sin\theta & \cos^2\theta & 0 \\ 0 & 0 & 0 & 1 \end{bmatrix}$$

On the other hand, the two rotations carried out in the reverse order—i.e., a rotation about the y-axis followed by an equal rotation about the x-axis, with $\theta = \emptyset$—yields

$$R = \begin{bmatrix} \cos\emptyset & 0 & -\sin\emptyset & 0 \\ 0 & 1 & 0 & 0 \\ \sin\emptyset & 0 & \cos\emptyset & 0 \\ 0 & 0 & 0 & 1 \end{bmatrix} \begin{bmatrix} 1 & 0 & 0 & 0 \\ 0 & \cos\theta & \sin\theta & 0 \\ 0 & -\sin\theta & \cos\theta & 0 \\ 0 & 0 & 0 & 1 \end{bmatrix}$$

$$= \begin{bmatrix} \cos\theta & \sin^2\theta & -\cos\theta\sin\theta & 0 \\ 0 & \cos\theta & \sin\theta & 0 \\ \sin\theta & -\cos\theta\sin\theta & \cos^2\theta & 0 \\ 0 & 0 & 0 & 1 \end{bmatrix}$$

Comparison of the two results shows that they are not the same. The fact that three-dimensional rotations are noncommutative must be kept in mind when more than one rotation is made.

Since generalized three-dimensional rotation is a very important capability, equations (7.10), (7.11), (7.12), (7.13), and (7.14) can be used as a basis for computer software. Such an algorithm is particularly useful for computer animations.

7.2 PERSPECTIVE VIEWS

When a perspective view of an object is created, the horizontal reference line is normally at eye level, as shown in Fig. 7.6. *Vanishing points* (VP) are those points on the horizon line or eye level at which parallel horizontal lines converge. We note that different sets of horizontal parallel lines will have different vanishing points. Lines which are parallel to one another but are not horizontal will converge to points which lie above or (TP) below the horizon line. These points are called *trace points* and are shown in Fig. 7.6.

7.2.1 Perspective Projection

A perspective projection is obtained by using similar triangles, as shown in Fig. 7.7. It follows that

$$\frac{y}{y_s} = \frac{f + z}{f}$$

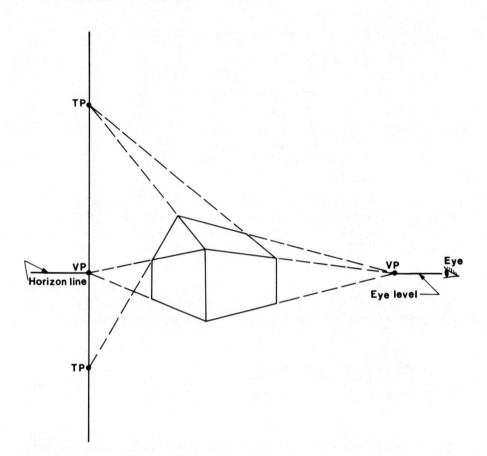

Figure 7.6 Trace points and vanishing points

and

$$\frac{x}{x_s} = \frac{f + z}{f}$$

so that screen coordinates are given by

$$x_s = \frac{fx}{f + z} \qquad \qquad (7.15)$$

and

$$y_s = \frac{fy}{f + z} \qquad \qquad (7.16)$$

In Fig. 7.7 the nontransformed point P is transformed to P_s by the above operations. The center of projection is located at

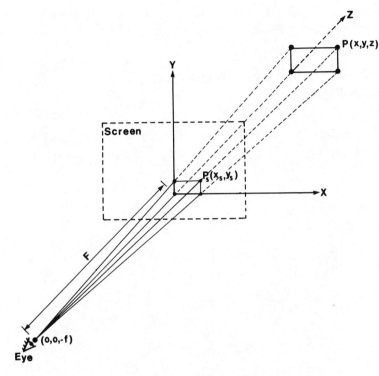

Figure 7.7 Perspective projection of a point

$[0\ 0\ -f]$ and the plane of projection is $z = 0$. Since the above operation produces no translation, the origin is unchanged and the xy and $x_s y_s$ coordinates share the same origin.

By increasing f we flatten out the image, and by decreasing f we increase the perspective. As $f \to \infty$, we approach a parallel projection and

$$x_s \to x$$

$$y_s \to y$$

The distance f should be chosen according to viewing parameters. These include the size of the object, the size of the projection screen, and the viewing distance. When viewing a screen display, the position of the viewpoint or eye is normally fixed. Thus, rather than moving the viewpoint to obtain an acceptable perspective view, it is common to manipulate the position and orientation of the object displayed on the screen. This will normally require one or more rotations and translations of the object.

7.2.2 Perspective Projection from a Point

It is possible to generalize equations (7.15) and (7.16) by placing a viewpoint at $(x_0, y_0, -f)$, in which case the screen

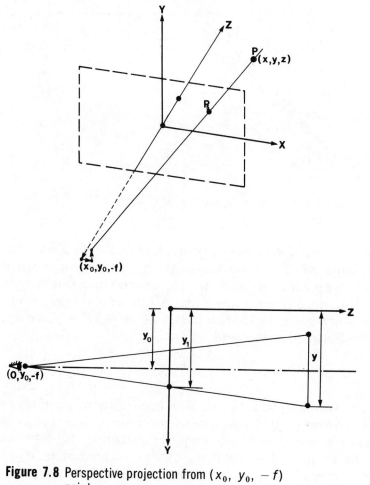

Figure 7.8 Perspective projection from $(x_0, y_0, -f)$ point

coordinates are related to the space coordinates as follows (see Fig. 7.8):

$$x_s = x_0 + (x - x_0)\frac{f}{f + z}$$

$$y_s = y_0 + (y - y_0)\frac{f}{f + z}$$

By simplifying, we get

$$x_s = \frac{x_0 z + xf}{f + z} \tag{7.17}$$

$$y_s = \frac{y_0 z + yf}{f + z} \tag{7.18}$$

A useful display technique can be derived from equations (7.17) and (7.18) by letting $y_0 = 0$ and x_0 take a positive and a negative value. This gives stereographic projection. The stereographic projection creates the illusion of depth and is used instead of the hidden line removal algorithm. Graphical outputs of engineering structures, such as bridges and towers, lend themselves nicely to stereographic projection. Also, the representation of three-dimensional arrangements, such as piping systems and architectural designs, can be improved by the use of stereographic projection.

7.2.3 Generalization of Perspective Projection

Consider the viewpoint of the observer at the point $(-f, -f, -f)$. Consider this observer looking toward the origin, and project onto the plane $(x + y + z = 0)$, as shown in Fig. 7.9.

Consider a point P on the object, with coordinates (x_p, y_p, z_p). The ray from $(-f, -f, -f)$ to (x_p, y_p, z_p) has on it the general point

$$\left.\begin{array}{l} x = -\lambda f + (1 - \lambda)x_p \\ y = -\lambda f + (1 - \lambda)y_p \\ z = -\lambda f + (1 - \lambda)z_p \end{array}\right\} \tag{7.19}$$

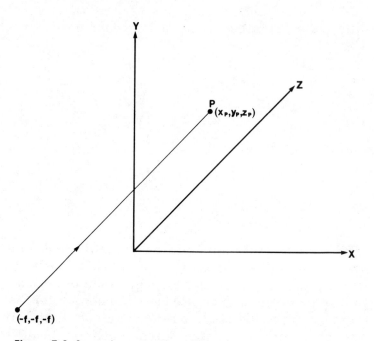

Figure 7.9 General perspective view

The intersection with $x + y + z = 0$ is given by substituting equations (7.19)

$$- 3\lambda f + (1 - \lambda)(x_p + y_p + z_p) = 0$$

or

$$\lambda = \frac{x_p + y_p + z_p}{3f + (x_p + y_p + z_p)} \qquad (7.20)$$

Hence, the coordinates of the point of the intersection with the plane $x + y + z = 0$ are found by substituting equation (7.20) in equations (7.19)

$$x = -f \frac{x_p + y_p + z_p}{3f + x_p + y_p + z_p} + x_p \frac{3f}{3f + x_p + y_p + z_p}$$

that is,

$$x = \frac{f(2x_p - y_p - z_p)}{3f + x_p + y_p + z_p}$$

Similarly, $\qquad\qquad\qquad\qquad\qquad\qquad\qquad\qquad\qquad$ **(7.21)**

$$y = \frac{f(2y_p - z_p - x_p)}{3f + x_p + y_p + z_p}$$

$$z = \frac{f(2z_p - x_p - y_p)}{3f + x_p + y_p + z_p}$$

The representation of this point for graphic purposes is achieved by setting up an axis system (x_s, y_s) for display purposes as shown in Fig. 7.10.

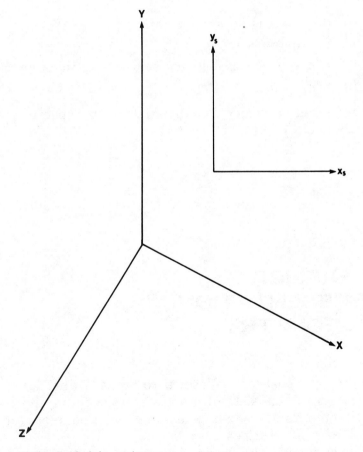

Figure 7.10 Axis system

then

$$x_s = (y - x) \cos 30°$$

$$= \frac{3\sqrt{3}\, f(y_p - x_p)}{2(3f + x_p + y_p + z_p)}$$

and

$$y_s = z - \frac{x + y}{2}$$

$$= \frac{3f(2z_p - x_p - y_p)}{2(3f + x_p + y_p + z_p)}$$

(7.22)

It should be noted that

(i) the z-axis is always vertical

(ii) f is arbitrary

(iii) $3f + x_p + y_p + z_p$ must not become zero; therefore, choose f accordingly.

For an isometric projection rather than perspective, we let $f \to \infty$; hence,

$$x_s = \frac{\sqrt{3}}{2}\,(y_p - x_p)$$

$$y_s = \frac{1}{2}\,(2z_p - x_p - y_p)$$

(7.23)

7.3 EXPLICIT REPRESENTATION OF GEOMETRY

For many purposes, it is useful to treat a line figure as a graph. A graph consists of a set of vertices and another set whose elements are edges, such that each edge is identified with a pair of vertices.

The connectivity matrix of vertices can be used to encode a graph numerically for computer storage.

The numerical information given by the connectivity matrix and the list of vertex coordinates is sufficient to draw a three-dimensional form. For example, using equations (7.15) and (7.16), a perspective view could be drawn of the form. This representation eliminates redundancy in the description of geometry. Each point appears only once in the vertex list which gives its coordinates; each line in the connectivity matrix gives information about the vertices which are connected to each other.

7.3.1 Sparse Matrix Technique

A disadvantage of the connectivity matrix technique is that it consumes excessive storage when the figure is large. For a figure composed of n points, a connectivity matrix of n^2 words is required. Since the matrix is symmetrical, some savings can be achieved by storing only the entries on one side of the diagonal. Much greater economies can be achieved by recognizing that the matrix will characteristically be very sparse—i.e., it will mostly consist of 0's. The efficient storage of large sparse matrices is a common problem in computing, and several techniques have been developed for this purpose.

One obvious approach is to exploit the property that, in principle, an entry can be represented by a single bit. A whole word is not needed. If individual bits of memory can be addressed, large savings result. For example, if the computer uses 60 bits, storage of a 600×600 binary matrix in words requires $600 \times 600 = 360K$ words. If stored as a bit pattern, only $600 \times 600/60 = 6K$ words are required. Storage requirements are cut by a factor of 60. Unfortunately, it is tedious to manipulate individual bits.

Considerable savings in storage can be achieved by storing only subscript pairs identifying the non-zero entries of the lower triangular matrix and noting that the diagonal term does not give any useful information (since it indicates only that the vertex is connected to itself). If we follow this scheme, then the connectivity matrix of Fig. 7.11(b) can be written as shown:

NCP	IROW	ICOL		NCP	IROW	ICOL
1	2	1		10	8	4
2	3	2		11	8	5
3	4	1		12	8	7
4	4	3		13	9	5
5	5	1		14	9	6
6	6	2		15	10	7
7	6	5		16	10	8
8	7	3		17	10	9
9	7	6				

NCP = Number of connection points
IROW = Row subscript
ICOL = Column subscript

Even though the connectivity matrix requires only 100 words of storage, its representation as a pair of subscripts reduces its storage requirement to 34 words. It should be noted that, although savings in storage are achieved by using vectors, a penalty has been paid on the utilization of CPU. The extra utilization of CPU occurs because the construction of IROW and ICOL is done automatically once the description of the geometry is given. For example, to represent the form shown in Fig. 7.11(a), the vertices defining the surfaces must be identified as shown below:

SURFACE	VERTEX 1	VERTEX 2	VERTEX 3	VERTEX 4
1	1	2	6	5
2	2	3	7	6
3	3	4	8	7
4	4	1	5	8
5	2	3	4	1
6	6	7	8	5
7	6	7	10	9
8	8	5	9	10
9	5	6	9	0
10	7	8	10	0

The zero entry in the vertex 4 means that the surface concerned is a triangle. To transform from the above matrix to the IROW and ICOL form, surfaces have to be defined in

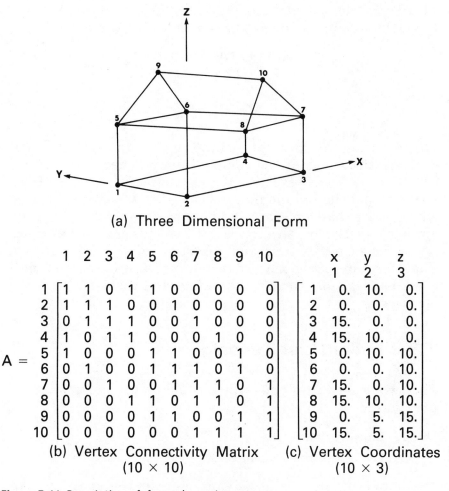

(a) Three Dimensional Form

$$A = \begin{array}{c} \\ 1 \\ 2 \\ 3 \\ 4 \\ 5 \\ 6 \\ 7 \\ 8 \\ 9 \\ 10 \end{array} \begin{array}{cccccccccc} 1 & 2 & 3 & 4 & 5 & 6 & 7 & 8 & 9 & 10 \\ \begin{bmatrix} 1 & 1 & 0 & 1 & 1 & 0 & 0 & 0 & 0 & 0 \\ 1 & 1 & 1 & 0 & 0 & 1 & 0 & 0 & 0 & 0 \\ 0 & 1 & 1 & 1 & 0 & 0 & 1 & 0 & 0 & 0 \\ 1 & 0 & 1 & 1 & 0 & 0 & 0 & 1 & 0 & 0 \\ 1 & 0 & 0 & 0 & 1 & 1 & 0 & 0 & 1 & 0 \\ 0 & 1 & 0 & 0 & 1 & 1 & 1 & 0 & 1 & 0 \\ 0 & 0 & 1 & 0 & 0 & 1 & 1 & 1 & 0 & 1 \\ 0 & 0 & 0 & 1 & 1 & 0 & 1 & 1 & 0 & 1 \\ 0 & 0 & 0 & 0 & 1 & 1 & 0 & 0 & 1 & 1 \\ 0 & 0 & 0 & 0 & 0 & 0 & 1 & 1 & 1 & 1 \end{bmatrix} \end{array}$$

$$\begin{array}{c} \\ 1 \\ 2 \\ 3 \\ 4 \\ 5 \\ 6 \\ 7 \\ 8 \\ 9 \\ 10 \end{array} \begin{array}{ccc} x & y & z \\ 1 & 2 & 3 \\ \begin{bmatrix} 0. & 10. & 0. \\ 0. & 0. & 0. \\ 15. & 0. & 0. \\ 15. & 10. & 0. \\ 0. & 10. & 10. \\ 0. & 0. & 10. \\ 15. & 0. & 10. \\ 15. & 10. & 10. \\ 0. & 5. & 15. \\ 15. & 5. & 15. \end{bmatrix} \end{array}$$

(b) Vertex Connectivity Matrix   (c) Vertex Coordinates
(10 × 10)   (10 × 3)

Figure 7.11 Description of forms by vertex connectivity matrix and vertex list of coordinates

terms of edges. For example, the first surface 1 2 6 5 define
the following connectivity matrix associated with it.

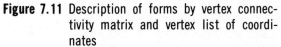

The connectivity matrix, being symmetric, is stored in pairs of vertices defining edges as ROW and COL vectors.

$$
\begin{array}{ccc}
\textbf{NCP} & \textbf{ROW} & \textbf{COL} \\
1 & & \\
2 & \begin{Bmatrix} 2 \\ 5 \\ 6 \\ 6 \end{Bmatrix} & \begin{Bmatrix} 1 \\ 1 \\ 2 \\ 5 \end{Bmatrix} \\
3 & & \\
4 & &
\end{array}
$$

This information can be stored in the vectors ROW and COL defining the edges of the complete form. There are several issues to be resolved. These are: the effective length of the vectors; and the redundancy checks—i.e., no edge should be stored more than once, as would be the case for the {2 1} edge arising from the fourth surface {2 3 4 1}. This means that there is an extensive search and insertion operation required. Therefore, if sparse matrix techniques are used, then efficient methods of storing, searching, and insertion must be employed.

7.3.2 Linked List Technique

The two other techniques which could be used to advantage are:

1. Linearly linked lists, and
2. Circular or ring structure lists.

The list structure has an advantage over the array type of structure in storing and insertion; however, the cost of searching is still comparable. The data structures of these lists are described in Chap. 5, and the reader is referred to this chapter for further information.

7.4 HIDDEN LINE ELIMINATION

The house shown in Fig. 7.12 includes the hidden lines. The inclusion of the hidden line without any differentiation of

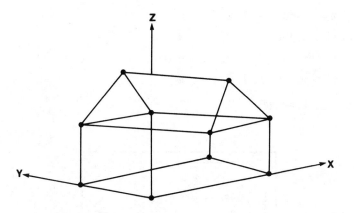

Figure 7.12 Wire frame diagram

other lines leads to a wire frame diagram. This diagram, although very simple to construct, store, and plot, leads to ambiguous interpretation of the picture. There are several techniques available to remove this ambiguity. One of the techniques used is the removal of the hidden lines. This technique requires considerable computation but is nevertheless useful for producing a finished diagram of the objects.

We can remove hidden lines from the wire frame diagram if we can determine just how much of a line segment is actually seen and how much is hidden. This amounts to the repeated solution of the following problem.

The problem is to determine, given a point (x', y', z') and a surface defined by n points $\{(x_i, y_i, z_i): i = 1, 2, 3, \ldots, n\}$, whether that point is, in fact, hidden by the surface.

To determine this, we apply some tests to the point-plane combination.

7.4.1 Min-Max Test

The first test, the *min-max test*, checks to see if the point in question is outside the rectangle enclosing the projected surface (since this is a 2-D question). If any one of the four following conditions hold, then the point is not hidden by the surface and no further tests are required. This test is used to dispense quickly with the clear-cut cases, and to save computer time. The conditions are:

1. $x' \geq x_i$ for $i = 1, 2, \ldots, n$
2. $x' \leq x_i$ for $i = 1, 2, \ldots, n$
3. $y' \geq y_i$ for $i = 1, 2, \ldots, n$
4. $y' \leq y_i$ for $i = 1, 2, \ldots, n$

_____ **Example:**

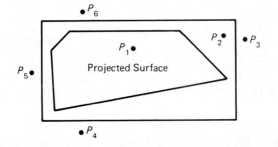

Note that points P_1 and P_2 fail all four conditions while P_3, P_4, P_5, and P_6 satisfy at least one of the four conditions.

7.4.2 The Dot-Product Test

If a point fails all four conditions of the min-max test, we go on to the dot-product test to determine whether the point in question is in front of or behind the plane containing the surface in question. In the first case, the point is seen, whereas in the second case it is possibly hidden.

Given three points $(x_1\, y_1\, z_1)$, $(x_2\, y_2\, z_2)$, and $(x_3\, y_3\, z_3)$ of the surface, this is sufficient to define the plane as follows: let

$$A = \begin{vmatrix} y_1 & z_1 & 1 \\ y_2 & z_2 & 1 \\ y_3 & z_3 & 1 \end{vmatrix} \qquad B = \begin{vmatrix} z_1 & x_1 & 1 \\ z_2 & x_2 & 1 \\ z_3 & x_2 & 1 \end{vmatrix}$$

$$C = \begin{vmatrix} x_1 & y_1 & 1 \\ x_2 & y_2 & 1 \\ x_3 & y_3 & 1 \end{vmatrix} \qquad D = \begin{vmatrix} x_1 & y_1 & 1 \\ x_2 & y_2 & 2 \\ x_3 & y_3 & 3 \end{vmatrix}$$

then we can define the plane with the following equation:

$$Ax + By + Cz + D = 0 \qquad \text{(3-point form)}$$

let our point be

$$(a, b, c)$$

then let

$$Q = (A\ B\ C\ D) \cdot (a\ b\ c\ 1)$$

where · denotes the dot product operation.

If $Q > 0$, then (a, b, c) is in front of the plane (i.e., seen).
If $Q = 0$, then (a, b, c) is in the plane.
If $Q < 0$, then (a, b, c) is behind the plane (possibly hidden).

_____ **Note:**

If $Q > 0$, the point is seen and no further tests are required. Otherwise, we go on to the third and final test.

7.4.3 The Polygon Test

This test is applied only if the previous two tests fail—that is, if the point is inside the rectangle enclosing the projected surface and the point is behind the plane containing the surface. This third test is in fact similar to test one but is much more exacting as it determines whether a point is inside or outside of a given polygon. This test can be best explained using diagrams.

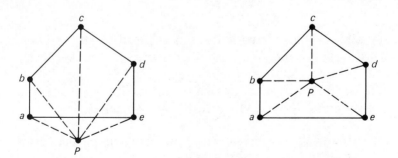

Let P be a point and $abcde$ be a polygon. Now define the angles

$$A_1 = \sphericalangle aPb,\ A_2 = \sphericalangle bPc,\ A_3 = \sphericalangle cPd$$
$$A_4 = \sphericalangle dPe,\ A_5 = \sphericalangle ePa$$

Now, if P is inside the polygon, then

$$\sum_{i=1}^{5} A_i \equiv 2\pi$$

if P is outside the polygon, then

$$\sum_{i=1}^{5} A_i < 2\pi$$

These angles may be easily computed since we are given the coordinates of all the points involved. (One way is the use of cosine law.) The above argument generalizes to the general case of an n-sided polygon.

Therefore, if

$$\sum_{i=1}^{n} A_i = 2\pi$$

then the point is inside the polygon and, because it also failed test two, the point is definitely hidden.

It should be noted that the algorithms presented here are very elementary and do not address many difficult issues. However, the algorithms presented do introduce an interested reader to the hidden line problem.

7.5 HIDDEN SURFACE REMOVAL

A very simple procedure is developed to find the surface orientation of the cube. We just need to take a vector dot product and proceed as described in Sec. 5.2. (See Fig. 7.13.)

Thus, the surface orientation algorithm could be used to draw only the edges of the front-facing surfaces.

(i)   If an edge is common to a front-facing and a back-facing surface, then it is an exterior edge.

(ii) If an edge is common to two front-facing surfaces, then it is an interior edge.

(iii) If an edge is common to two back-facing surfaces, then it is invisible.

For details on data structures for the cube, Sec. 5.2 should be consulted. We emphasize that there are several advanced procedures which could be used for hidden surface removal. In recent times, more attention has been paid to this problem than the hidden line problem. Those who are interested in this subject are advised to read about algorithms for hidden surface removal developed by investigators working in raster scan graphics.

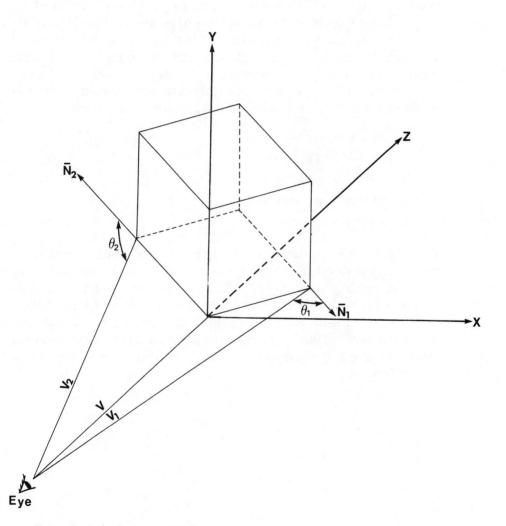

Figure 7.13 Surface orientation

7.6 COMPUTER PROGRAM TO DRAW A WIRE FRAME DIAGRAM OF A HOUSE

A sample program to draw a wire frame diagram of a house is presented. This program calls on a series of subprograms from the computer library called the *PLOT10 Library*. The program and PLOT10 subprograms are both written in FOR-TRAN language and were implemented on Control Data Corporation's Cyber 170 computer. This program illustrates how the algorithms developed in Chap. 7 could be implemented on a computer. The basic program is written for the CDC Cyber 170 computer but, with minor modifications, could be implemented on any micro, mini, or large computer, such as:

1. Alpha Micro
2. DEC PDP-11
3. HP 2000 and 3000 series
4. IBM 370 and 3000 series
5. CDC Cyber series

The program is structured and extensively commented to be easily understood. The figure shown below is the output from the Tektronix hardcopy unit. The picture of the house is ambiguous for several reasons. The first one is that the hidden lines are not removed. The second is that equations (7.15) and (7.16) are derived with a particular position of the axis. Several rotations are required to achieve a suitable perspective view of the house.

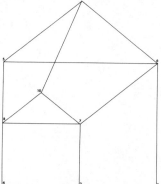

```
      PROGRAM HOUSE(HOUSDT,OUTPUT,INPUT=HOUSDT)
***********************************************************************
*     INITIALIZE AND READ IN DATA                                    *
***********************************************************************
      DIMENSION X(10,3),NSURF(8,4),IROW(100),ICOL(100),INDEX1(5)
     * ,INDEX2(4),NODE(2)
      LOGICAL LABELD(100)
      INPUT=5LINPUT
      REWIND INPUT
      DATA INDEX1/1,2,3,4,1/
      DATA INDEX2/1,2,3,1/
      READ *,N,M,((NSURF(I,J),J=1,4),I=1,N)
      READ *,((X(I,J),J=1,3),I=1,M)
***********************************************************************
*   INITIALIZE ELEMENT COUNTER AND PUT INITIAL VALUES IN             *
*   ICOL AND IROW.                                                   *
***********************************************************************
      L=1
      IROW(1)=NSURF(1,1)
      ICOL(1)=NSURF(1,2)
***********************************************************************
*     OBTAIN EDGES FOR THE FOUR SIDED SURFACES, CALL ON              *
*     SUBROUTINE SEARCH TO CHECK IF EDGE IS ALREADY DECLARED.        *
***********************************************************************
      DO 1 I=1,6
        DO 1 J=1,4
          NODE(1)=NSURF(I,INDEX1(J))
          NODE(2)=NSURF(I,INDEX1(J+1))
          CALL SEARCH(NODE,L,ICOL,IROW)
 1    CONTINUE
***********************************************************************
*     OBTAIN EDGES FOR THE THREE SIDED SURFACES                      *
***********************************************************************
      DO 2 I=7,8
        DO 2 J=1,3
          NODE(1)=NSURF(I,INDEX2(J))
          NODE(2)=NSURF(I,INDEX2(J+1))
          CALL SEARCH(NODE,L,ICOL,IROW)
 2    CONTINUE
***********************************************************************
*     PLOT OUT THE DATA                                              *
***********************************************************************
      CALL PLOT(L,ICOL,IROW,X)
      STOP
      END
```

```
      SUBROUTINE SEARCH(NODE,L,ICOL,IROW)
      DIMENSION NODE(2),ICOL(100),IROW(100)
***********************************************************************
*     CHECK IF EDGE IS ALREADY IN IROW AND ICOL. "J" IS THE          *
*     INDEX USED TO SEARCH THE ARRAYS FROM THE BOTTOM UP.            *
***********************************************************************
      DO 1 K=1,L
         J=L-K+1
         IF ((NODE(1).EQ.ICOL(J)).AND.(NODE(2).EQ.IROW(J))) RETURN
         IF ((NODE(2).EQ.ICOL(J)).AND.(NODE(1).EQ.IROW(J))) RETURN
1     CONTINUE
***********************************************************************
*     IF IT MAKES IT THIS FAR THEN THE EDGE IS NOT IN THE ARRAYS     *
*     THEREFORE ENTER IT IN AND INCREASE THE ELEMENT COUNT.          *
***********************************************************************
      L=L+1
      IROW(L)=NODE(1)
      ICOL(L)=NODE(2)
      RETURN
      END


      SUBROUTINE PLOT(N,ICOL,IROW,X)
***********************************************************************
*     THIS ROUTINE TAKES IROW AND ICOL AND FINDS THEIR              *
*     COORDINATES OF THE EDGES AND CALCULATES A 2-D VIEW            *
*     OF THE OBJECT USING THE FOLLOWING EQUATIONS:                  *
*                    X'=F*X/F+Z                                      *
*                    Y'=F*Y/F+Z                                      *
***********************************************************************
      DIMENSION ICOL(100),IROW(100),X(100,3)
      LOGICAL LABELD(100)
      DO 2 I=1,100
         LABELD(I)=.FALSE.
2     CONTINUE
      F=10.0
      CALL INITT(30)
      CALL VWINDO(0.,15.,0.,15.)
      DO 1 I=1,N
         X1=F*X(IROW(I),1)/(F+X(IROW(I),2))
         Y1=F*X(IROW(I),3)/(F+X(IROW(I),2))
         X2=F*X(ICOL(I),1)/(F+X(ICOL(I),2))
         Y2=F*X(ICOL(I),3)/(F+X(ICOL(I),2))
         CALL MOVEA(X1,Y1)
         CALL DRAWA(X2,Y2)
         CALL LABEL(X1,Y1,IROW(I),LABELD)
         CALL LABEL(X2,Y2,ICOL(I),LABELD)
1     CONTINUE
      CALL FINITT(0,767)
      RETURN
      END
```

```
      SUBROUTINE LABEL(X,Y,N,LABELD)
*******************************************************************
*     THIS ROUTINE LABELS THE NODES. IF THE NODE IS ALREADY      *
*     LABELED THEN FLOW RETURNS TO SUBROUTINE PLOT               *
*******************************************************************
      LOGICAL LABELD(100)
      IF(LABELD(N)) RETURN
      LABELD(N)=.TRUE.
      CALL WINCOT(X+.10,Y+.2,IX,IY)
      CALL MOVABS(IX,IY)
      CALL ANCHO(N+48)
      CALL MOVEA(X,Y)
      RETURN
      END
```

7.7 COMPUTER PROGRAM TO DRAW A PERSPECTIVE VIEW WITH HIDDEN LINE REMOVED

In the previous computer code, neither were suitable rotations applied to the perspective figure nor were hidden lines removed from the picture. The following program achieves both of these. The three tests described in Sec. 7.4 are used and general formulation of a perspective view given by equation (7.22) is employed. Two outputs are generated, one with hidden lines is shown in the dotted form. These are shown in Fig. 7.14(a) and (b). Unfortunately, the partially hidden lines cannot be removed by the simple algorithms presented in this chapter.

SUMMARY

In this chapter, several concepts relevant to three-dimensional graphics, such as homogeneous coordinates, 3-D transformation, perspective projection, hidden line removal, and hidden surface removal, are developed. The description of these concepts is elementary in nature and is inclined toward vector graphics rather than raster graphics. From an engineering point of view, vector graphics is still the popular way to do computer graphics, and this explains the emphasis used in this text. The algorithms developed could also be used for raster scan graphics.

Finally, two FORTRAN programs are given at the end of the chapter which employ the concepts developed in the chapter on three-dimensional graphics. The first program draws a wire frame diagram of a house, and the second program draws a perspective view with hidden lines removed.

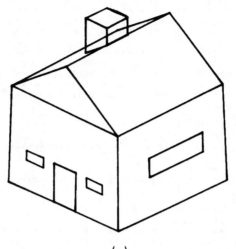

(a)

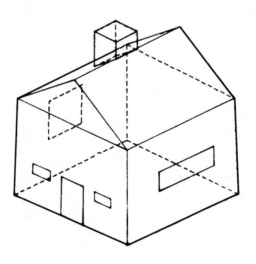

(b)

Figure 7.14 **(a)** House with hidden lines removed (partially hidden lines not removed). **(b)** House with hidden lines shown as dotted (partially hidden lines not removed)

```
      PROGRAM HOUSE (HOUSDT,OUTPUT,INPUT=HOUSDT)
********************************************************************
*   THIS PROGRAM PLOTS A HOUSE ON THE TEKTRONIX TERMINAL AND      *
*   THEN ROTATES IT 90 DEGREES AT A TIME AROUND THE VERTICAL      *
*   AXIS.                                                         *
********************************************************************
      DIMENSION X(4,300),NSURF(50,4),IROWS(100),ICOLS(100),IROWD(100)
     * ,ICOLD(100),INDEX1(5),INDEX2(4),NODE(2),SNORMAL(4,50),ROTATE(4,4)
     * ,SCALE(4,4),TRANS1(4,4),TRANS2(4,4),PITCH(4,4),ROLL(4,4)
     * ,YAW(4,4),X1(4,300),TEMP(4,4),AM(4,4),TEMP1(4,4),TEMP2(4,4)
     * ,BNORMAL(4,50)
      LOGICAL HIDD
********************************************************************
*   INITIALIZE DATA AND PLOT ROUTINES                            *
********************************************************************
      DATA INDEX1/1,2,3,4,1/
      DATA INDEX2/1,2,3,1/
      DATA S,A,B,C,T1X,T1Y,T1Z,T2X,T2Y,T2Z/1.,0.,0.,0.,0.,0.,0.,0.
     * ,0.,0./
      F=100.0
      CALL INITT(30)
      CALL VWINDO(-18.,38.,-15.,40.)
********************************************************************
*  READ IN THE SURFACES, POINTS AND THE NORMALS TO THE SURFACES  *
********************************************************************
      READ *,N,L,((NSURF(I,J),J=1,4),I=1,N)
      READ *,((X1(I,J),I=1,4),J=1,L)
      READ *,((BNORMAL(I,J),I=1,4),J=1,N)
********************************************************************
*   INTIALIZE DUMMY ELEMENTS IN THE VECTORS                      *
********************************************************************
      IROWS(1)=-100
      ICOLS(1)=-100
      IROWD(1)=-100
      ICOLD(1)=-100
```

```
***************************************************************
*   DRAW THE HOUSE ROTATING IT 90 DEGREES EACH TIME          *
***************************************************************
      DO 10 II=45,405,90
        LS=1
        LD=1
        J=II-45
        C=FLOAT(J)
***************************************************************
*   TRANSFORM THE POINTS AND THE NORMALS                     *
***************************************************************
        CALL TRANS(S,A,B,C,T1X,T1Y,T1Z,T2X,T2Y,T2Z,X1,X,L)
        CALL TRANS(S,A,B,C,T1X,T1Y,T1Z,T2X,T2Y,T2Z,BNORMAL,SNORMAL,N)
***************************************************************
*   FOR EACH SURFACE DETERMINE IF IT IS HIDDEN OR NOT.       *
*   IF IT IS HIDDEN PLACE THE EDGE IN "IROWD" AND "ICOLD"    *
*   IF IT IS VISIBLE PLACE THE EDGE IN "IROWS" AND "ICOLS"   *
*   PERFORM THIS PROCEDURE FOR BOTH THE FOUR SIDED SURFACES  *
*   AND THE THREE SIDED SURFACES.                            *
***************************************************************
        DO 1 I=1,16
          CALL HIDDEN(F,I,X,NSURF(I,1),HIDD,SNORMAL)
          IF (HIDD) THEN
            DO 2 J=1,4
              NODE(1)=NSURF(I,INDEX1(J))
              NODE(2)=NSURF(I,INDEX1(J+1))
              CALL SEARCH(NODE,LD,ICOLD,IROWD)
2           CONTINUE
          ELSE
            DO 3 J=1,4
              NODE(1)=NSURF(I,INDEX1(J))
              NODE(2)=NSURF(I,INDEX1(J+1))
              CALL SEARCH(NODE,LS,ICOLS,IROWS)
3           CONTINUE
          END IF
1       CONTINUE
        DO 4 I=17,18
          CALL HIDDEN(F,I,X,NSURF(I,1),HIDD,SNORMAL)
          IF (HIDD) THEN
            DO 5 J=1,3
              NODE(1)=NSURF(I,INDEX2(J))
              NODE(2)=NSURF(I,INDEX2(J+1))
              CALL SEARCH(NODE,LD,ICOLD,IROWD)
5           CONTINUE
          ELSE
            DO 6 J=1,3
              NODE(1)=NSURF(I,INDEX2(J))
              NODE(2)=NSURF(I,INDEX2(J+1))
              CALL SEARCH(NODE,LS,ICOLS,IROWS)
6           CONTINUE
          END IF
4       CONTINUE
***************************************************************
*   CALL SUBROUTINE PLOT TO PLOT OUT THE HOUSE               *
***************************************************************
        CALL PLOT(LS,LD,ICOLD,ICOLS,IROWD,IROWS,X,F)
        CALL TINPUT(K)
        CALL NEWPAG
10      CONTINUE
        CALL FINITT(0,767)
        STOP
        END
```

```
      SUBROUTINE HIDDEN(FOCAL,N,X,P1,HIDD,SNORMAL)
*****************************************************************
*   THIS ROUTINE DETERMINES IF A SURFACE IS VISIBLE OR NOT    *
*****************************************************************
      REAL FP(3),F(3),X(4,300),SNORMAL(4,50)
      INTEGER P1
      LOGICAL HIDD
      HIDD=.FALSE.
      F(1)=-FOCAL
      F(2)=-FOCAL
      F(3)=-FOCAL
*****************************************************************
*   DETERMINE THE VECTOR FROM THE FOCAL POINT TO A POINT      *
*   ON THE SURFACE IN QUESTION                                *
*****************************************************************
      DO 10 I=1,3
         FP(I)=X(I,P1)-F(I)
10    CONTINUE
      DOT=0.0
*****************************************************************
*   DO THE DOT PRODUCT ON THE FOCAL VECTOR AND THE NORMAL     *
*   VECTOR TO THE SURFACE                                     *
*****************************************************************
      DO 20 I=1,3
         DOT=DOT+FP(I)*SNORMAL(I,N)
20    CONTINUE
*****************************************************************
*   IF THE DOT PRODUCT IS LESS THAN 0 THE THE SURFACE IS      *
*   HIDDEN                                                    *
*****************************************************************
      IF (DOT.LT.0.) HIDD=.TRUE.
      RETURN
      END


      SUBROUTINE SEARCH(NODE,L,ICOL,IROW)
*****************************************************************
*   THIS ROUTINE DOES A LINEAR SEARCH FROM THE BOTTOM UP ON   *
*   THE VECTORS ICOL AND IROW.                                *
*****************************************************************
      DIMENSION NODE(2),ICOL(100),IROW(100)
*****************************************************************
*   CHECK IF THE EDGE IS ALREADY IN IROW AND ICOL. "J" IS THE *
*   INDEX USED TO SEARCH THE ARRAYS FROM THE BOTTTOM UP       *
*****************************************************************
      DO 10 K=1,L
         J=L-K+1
         IF ((NODE(1).EQ.ICOL(J)).AND.(NODE(2).EQ.IROW(J))) RETURN
         IF ((NODE(2).EQ.ICOL(J)).AND.(NODE(1).EQ.IROW(J))) RETURN
10    CONTINUE
*****************************************************************
*   IF IT MAKES IT THIS FAR THEN THE EDGE IS NOT IN THE ARRAY *
*   THERFORE ENTER IT IN AND INCREASE THE ELEMENT COUNT       *
*****************************************************************
      L=L+1
      IROW(L)=NODE(1)
      ICOL(L)=NODE(2)
      RETURN
      END
```

```
      SUBROUTINE PLOT(N1,N2,ICOLD,ICOLS,IROWD,IROWS,X,F)
*******************************************************************
*   THIS ROUTINE CALCULATES THE 2-D VIEW OF THE HOUSE USING      *
*   THE X, Y, AND Z COORDINATES OF THE POINTS. HIDDEN LINES      *
*   ARE DRAWN IN AS DASHED LINES.                                *
*******************************************************************
      DIMENSION ICOLD(100),ICOLS(100),IROWD(100),IROWS(100),X(4,300)
*******************************************************************
*   CALCULATE THE 2-D VIEW OF THE HOUSE AND PLOT THE VISIBLE     *
*   LINES.                                                       *
*******************************************************************
      DO 10 I=2,N1
      XP1=X(1,IROWS(I))
      YP1=X(3,IROWS(I))
      ZP1=X(2,IROWS(I))
      XP2=X(1,ICOLS(I))
      YP2=X(3,ICOLS(I))
      ZP2=X(2,ICOLS(I))
      X1=3.0*F*SQRT(3.0)*(YP1-XP1)/(2.0*(3.0*F+XP1+YP1+ZP1))
      Y1=3.0*F*(2.0*ZP1-XP1-YP1)/(2.0*(3.0*F+XP1+YP1+ZP1))
      X2=3.0*F*SQRT(3.0)*(YP2-XP2)/(2.0*(3.0*F+XP2+YP2+ZP2))
      Y2=3.0*F*(2.0*ZP2-XP2-YP2)/(2.0*(3.0*F+XP2+YP2+ZP2))
      CALL MOVEA(X1,Y1)
      CALL DRAWA(X2,Y2)
  10  CONTINUE
*******************************************************************
*   CALCULATE AND PLOT THE HIDDEN LINES.                         *
*******************************************************************
      DO 20 I=2,N2
      XP1=X(1,IROWD(I))
      YP1=X(3,IROWD(I))
      ZP1=X(2,IROWD(I))
      XP2=X(1,ICOLD(I))
      YP2=X(3,ICOLD(I))
      ZP2=X(2,ICOLD(I))
      X1=3.0*F*SQRT(3.0)*(YP1-XP1)/(2.0*(3.0*F+XP1+YP1+ZP1))
      Y1=3.0*F*(2.0*ZP1-XP1-YP1)/(2.0*(3.0*F+XP1+YP1+ZP1))
      X2=3.0*F*SQRT(3.0)*(YP2-XP2)/(2.0*(3.0*F+XP2+YP2+ZP2))
      Y2=3.0*F*(2.0*ZP2-XP2-YP2)/(2.0*(3.0*F+XP2+YP2+ZP2))
      CALL MOVEA(X1,Y1)
      CALL DASHA(X2,Y2,3)
  20  CONTINUE
      RETURN
      END
```

```
       SURROUTINE TRANS(S,A,B,C,T1X,T1Y,T1Z,T2X,T2Y,T2Z,X1,X,N)
*************************************************************************
*    THIS ROUTINE IS THE DRIVER FOR THE TRANSFORMATIONS               *
*************************************************************************
       REAL ROTATE(4,4),PITCH(4,4),ROLL(4,4),YAW(4,4),TRANS1(4,4)
     * ,TRANS2(4,4),SCALE(4,4),X1(4,300),X(4,300),AM(4,4),TEMP1(4,4)
     * ,TEMP2(4,4),TEMP(4,4)
       CALL ROTATEM(A,B,C,ROTATE)
       CALL TRANSM(T1X,T1Y,T1Z,TRANS1)
       CALL TRANSM(T2X,T2Y,T2Z,TRANS2)
       CALL SCALEM(S,SCALE)
       CALL MATMUL(4,4,ROTATE,TRANS2,TEMP1)
       CALL MATMUL(4,4,TRANS1,TEMP1,TEMP2)
       CALL MATMUL(4,4,SCALE,TEMP2,AM)
       CALL MATMUL(300,N,AM,X1,X)
       RETURN
       END



       SURROUTINE MATMUL(MAX,N,A,B,C)
*************************************************************************
*    THIS ROUTINE DOES THE MATRIX MULTIPLICATION                      *
*************************************************************************
       REAL A(4,4),B(4,MAX),C(4,MAX)
       DO 1 I=1,4
         DO 1 J=1,N
           C(I,J)=0.0
           DO 1 K=1,4
             C(I,J)=C(I,J)+A(I,K)*B(K,J)
   1   CONTINUE
       RETURN
       END



       SURROUTINE TRANSM(TX,TY,TZ,TRANSL)
*************************************************************************
*    THIS ROUTINE PRODUCES THE TRANSLATION MATRIXES                   *
*************************************************************************
       REAL TRANSL(4,4)
       DO 10 I=1,4
         DO 10 J=1,4
           TRANSL(I,J)=0.0
           IF (I.EQ.J) TRANSL(I,J)=1.0
  10   CONTINUE
       TRANSL(1,4)=TX
       TRANSL(2,4)=TY
       TRANSL(3,4)=TZ
       RETURN
       END
```

```
      SUBROUTINE ROTATEM(A,B,C,ROTATE)
*****************************************************************
*    THIS ROUTINE PRODUCES THE ROTATION MATRIX                 *
*****************************************************************
      REAL PITCH(4,4),ROLL(4,4),YAW(4,4),ROTATE(4,4),TEMP(4,4)
      A1=(A*3.141592654)/180.
      B1=(B*3.141592654)/180.
      C1=(C*3.141592654)/180.
      DO 10 I=1,4
        DO 10 J=1,4
          ROLL(I,J)=0.0
          PITCH(I,J)=0.0
          YAW(I,J)=0.0
          IF (I.EQ.J) THEN
            ROLL(I,J)=1.0
            PITCH(I,J)=1.0
            YAW(I,J)=1.0
          END IF
10    CONTINUE
      ROLL(1,1)=COS(A1)
      ROLL(1,2)=SIN(A1)
      ROLL(2,1)=-SIN(A1)
      ROLL(2,2)=COS(A1)
      PITCH(2,2)=COS(B1)
      PITCH(2,3)=SIN(B1)
      PITCH(3,2)=-SIN(B1)
      PITCH(3,3)=COS(B1)
      YAW(1,1)=COS(C1)
      YAW(1,3)=SIN(C1)
      YAW(3,1)=-SIN(C1)
      YAW(3,3)=COS(C1)
      CALL MATMUL(4,4,PITCH,YAW,TEMP)
      CALL MATMUL(4,4,ROLL,TEMP,ROTATE)
      RETURN
      END



      SUBROUTINE SCALEM(S,SCALE)
*****************************************************************
*    THIS ROUTINE PRODUCES THE SCALE MATRIX                    *
*****************************************************************
      REAL SCALE(4,4)
      DO 10 I=1,4
        DO 10 J=1,4
          SCALE(I,J)=0.0
          IF (I.EQ.J) SCALE(I,J)=S
10    CONTINUE
      SCALE(4,4)=1.0
      RETURN
      END
```

Data

```
18  38
1   2   6   5
2   3   7   6
3   7   8   4
4   1   5   8
7   6   9  10
8   5   9  10
11  12  13  14
15  16  17  18
19  20  21  22
23  24  25  26
27  28  29  30
31  32  33  34
32  35  36  33
35  38  37  36
38  31  34  37
34  33  36  37
5   6   9   0
7   8  10   0
```

Surfaces (NSURF)

```
0.   0.    1.   1.
1.   0.    0.   1.
0.   0.   -1.   1.
-1.  0.    0.   1.
-1.  1.    0.   1.
1.   1.    0.   1.
0.   0.    1.   1.
0.   0.    1.   1.
0.   0.    1.   1.
-1.  0.    0.   1.
1.   0.    0.   1.
0.   0.    1.   1.
1.   0.    0.   1.
0.   0.   -1.   1.
-1.  0.    0.   1.
0.   1.    0.   1.
0.   0.    1.   1.
0.   0.   -1.   1.
```

Normals (BNORMAL)

```
0.    0.   -0.   1.
10.   0.   -0.   1.
10.   0.  -10.   1.
0.    0.  -10.   1.
0.   10.   -0.   1.
10.  10.   -0.   1.
10.  10.  -10.   1.
0.   10.  -10.   1.
5.   15.   -0.   1.
5.   15.  -10.   1.
4.    0.   -0.   1.
6.    0.   -0.   1.
6.    4.   -0.   1.
4.    4.   -0.   1.
1.5   3.   -0.   1.
3.    3.   -0.   1.
3.    4.   -0.   1.
1.5   4.   -0.   1.
7.    3.   -0.   1.
8.5   3.   -0.   1.
8.5   4.   -0.   1.
7.    4.   -0.   1.
0.    4.   -8.   1.
0.    4.   -3.   1.
0.    6.   -3.   1.
0.    6.   -8.   1.
10.   4.   -6.   1.
10.   4.   -3.   1.
10.   8.   -3.   1.
10.   8.   -6.   1.
5.   15.   -4.   1.
7.   13.   -4.   1.
7.   17.   -4.   1.
5.   17.   -4.   1.
7.   13.   -6.   1.
7.   17.   -6.   1.
5.   17.   -6.   1.
5.   15.   -6.   1.
```

Vertices (XI)

REFERENCES

Rogers, D. F. and Adams, A. J., *Mathematical Elements for Computer Graphics* (New York: McGraw-Hill Book Company, 1976).

Ryan, D. L., *Computer Aided Graphics and Design* (New York: Marcel Dekker, Inc., 1979).

Newmann, W. M. and Sproull, R. F., *Principles of Interactive Computer Graphics* (New York: McGraw-Hill Book Company, 1979).

Roberts, L. G., "Homogeneous Matrix Representation and Manipulation of N-Dimensional Constructs," Document MS1405, Lincoln Laboratory, MIT, Cambridge, Massachusetts, May 1965.

Jaeger, L. G., *Cartesian Tensors in Engineering Science* (London, England: Pergamon Press Ltd., 1966).

8
APPLICATION OF COMPUTER GRAPHICS TO ENGINEERING SCIENCE

8.1 INTRODUCTION

The *finite element method* is a very useful and general method for solving engineering problems concerning structural mechanics, electromagnetism, heat transfer, fluid flow, and other types of field problems. Essentially in this method, field problems reduce to the minimization of the integral I given in equation (8.1).

$$ I = \int \int \left[\frac{1}{2} \left\{ \left(\frac{\partial \emptyset}{\partial x} \right)^2 + \left(\frac{\partial \emptyset}{\partial y} \right)^2 \right\} - Q\emptyset \right] dx\,dy \qquad \text{(8.1)} $$

where $\emptyset$ is the unknown function.

Q is a known, specified constant or function of x and y. The reader can verify using the Euler-Lagrange theorem that the equivalent formulation to that of minimizing the integral I is to solve the partial differential equation (8.2).

$$\frac{\partial^2 \emptyset}{\partial x^2} + \frac{\partial^2 \emptyset}{\partial y^2} + Q = \emptyset \qquad (8.2)$$

The minimization procedure is accomplished by dividing the solid continuum of the physical problem into many finite discrete elements, sometimes hundreds or thousands. These elements may be triangles, rectangles, or curvilinear shapes (in two dimensions). Once the choice of an element is made, the characteristics of this element can be defined and equations derived to describe mathematically the local behavior of the elements. Summing these equations and applying boundary conditions of the problem yield a large system of linear equations which can be solved with acceptable accuracy, using computer techniques. The end result is a set of nodal values for the unknown quantities in question, whether they be velocities, temperatures, voltages, or displacements.

One drawback of the finite element method is the large amount of data needed to describe the problem domain. The

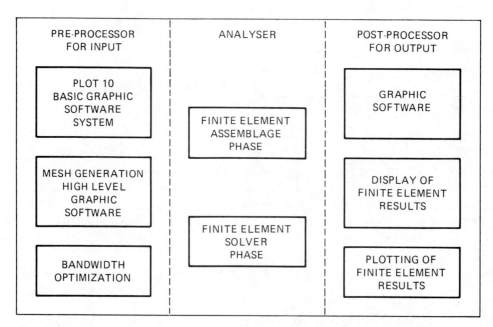

Figure 8.1

finite element method requires that the domain be divided into a finite number of elements. The elements must be numbered and the coordinates of each node in the mesh must be known. Generating the data by hand is not only slow, it increases the probability of human error, which can be difficult to detect. An automatic or semi-automatic method of mesh generation has the advantage of saving time; also, if interactive graphics is used as an aid in domain description and to display the finished mesh at each stage, the chance of a human error going undetected is virtually eliminated.

This chapter describes the total finite element system, as shown in Fig. 8.1, but particular attention is paid to computer graphic techniques which were used to preprocess and postprocess data interfaced with the Finite Element Analyzer Program.

8.2 BASIC FORMULATION

Consider a domain as shown in Fig. 8.2 on which the integral equation (8.1) is valid. This domain is subdivided into triangu-

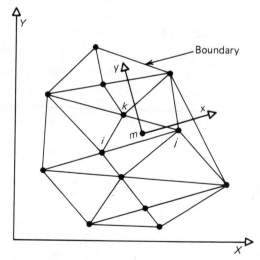

Figure 8.2

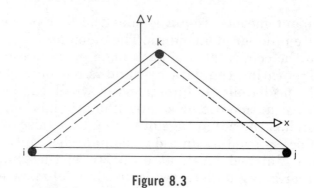

Figure 8.3

lar elements. This allows minimization of equation (8.1) on a much smaller domain, in this case a triangular element.

A triangular element m is isolated from the domain. The geometry of the triangle m is fixed according to the coordinates of i, j, and k nodes (vertices). Two axes are defined: XY are global axes and xy are local or attached axes to the centroid of the triangular element. Recall that the aim is to determine a function $\emptyset$ such that it minimizes equation (8.1) and will take numerical values $\emptyset_i \, \emptyset_j \, \emptyset_k$ on triangle m. Thus, labels i, j, and k are important, because these fix the geometry of triangle m and identify unknown values of function $\emptyset$ at i, j, and k.

(i) Element characteristic _____

Consider the triangular element m as shown in Fig. 8.3.

It is assumed that the function $\emptyset$ will be approximated by a linear interpolation function on the triangle m as

$$\phi = \mathbf{F}\underline{\delta}$$

$$\sim \, = \Rightarrow \text{row or matrix}$$

$$- \, = \Rightarrow \text{column}$$

where

$$\mathbf{F} = \frac{1}{2A}\left[(a_i + b_ix + c_iy)(a_j + b_jx + c_jy)(a_k + b_kx + c_ky)\right]$$

and

$$\underline{\delta} = \begin{Bmatrix} \emptyset_i \\ \emptyset_j \\ \emptyset_k \end{Bmatrix}$$

and

$$a_i = x_j y_k - x_k y_j \quad b_i = y_j - y_k \quad c_i = x_k - x_j$$
$$a_j = x_k y_i - x_i y_k \quad b_j = y_k - y_i \quad c_j = x_i - x_k$$
$$a_k = x_i y_j - x_j y_i \quad b_k = y_i - y_j \quad c_k = x_j - x_i$$

$$A = \text{area of triangle } m$$

and (x_i, y_i), (x_j, y_j), (x_k, y_k) are the local coordinates of the nodes i, j, and k.

Using equation (8.2),

$$\begin{Bmatrix} \dfrac{\partial \emptyset}{\partial x} \\[2mm] \dfrac{\partial \emptyset}{\partial y} \end{Bmatrix} = \frac{1}{2A} \begin{bmatrix} b_i & b_j & b_k \\ c_i & c_j & c_k \end{bmatrix} \begin{Bmatrix} \emptyset_i \\ \emptyset_j \\ \emptyset_k \end{Bmatrix}$$

or

$$\begin{Bmatrix} \dfrac{\partial \emptyset}{\partial x} \\[2mm] \dfrac{\partial \emptyset}{\partial y} \end{Bmatrix} = \mathbf{B} \underline{\delta} \tag{8.3}$$

We could write equation (8.1) in a convenient form

$$I = \frac{1}{2} \int \int \begin{bmatrix} \dfrac{\partial \emptyset}{\partial x} & \dfrac{\partial \emptyset}{\partial y} \end{bmatrix} \begin{Bmatrix} \dfrac{\partial \emptyset}{\partial x} \\[2mm] \dfrac{\partial \emptyset}{\partial y} \end{Bmatrix} dx dy - \int \int Q \emptyset dx dy$$

Substituting equation (8.3) and noting that the elements are constant and assuming a constant function Q, we obtain

$$I = \frac{1}{2} \underline{\delta}^T \mathbf{K} \underline{\delta} - \mathbf{R}^T \underline{\delta} \tag{8.4}$$

where

$$\mathbf{K} = \int \int \mathbf{B}^T \mathbf{B} \, dx dy$$

hence,

$$K = \frac{1}{4A} \begin{bmatrix} b_i^2 + c_i^2 & b_i b_j + c_i c_j & b_i b_k + c_i c_k \\ & b_i^2 + c_j^2 & b_j b_k + c_j c_k \\ \text{Symmetric} & & b_k^2 + c_k^2 \end{bmatrix}$$

$$R^T = \frac{QA}{3} \begin{bmatrix} 1 & 1 & 1 \end{bmatrix}$$

We note the following properties of a triangle

$$\iint dxdy = \text{Area of triangle} = A$$

$$\iint xdxdy = \frac{A}{3}(x_i + x_j + x_k) = 0$$

$$\iint ydxdy = \frac{A}{3}(y_i + y_j + y_k) = 0$$

Lastly, we find minimum of I by satisfying the equation

$$\frac{\partial I}{\partial \delta} = 0 \tag{8.5}$$

This gives

$$R = \mathbf{K}\underline{\delta} \tag{8.6}$$

In equation (8.6), we have transformed a continuum formulation [given by equation (8.1)] into a numerical formulation using the finite element approach.

(ii) Assembly of system equation _____

Equation (8.6) is valid for all elements and is used for all elements by suitably substituting their coordinates and node labels. These equations are added to give the system equation

$$R_s = K_s \underline{\delta}_s \tag{8.7}$$

where

$$R_s = \sum_{j=1}^{n} R$$

$$K_s = \sum_{j=1}^{n} K$$

We note that n = number of elements and $\underline{\delta}_s$ = unknown values of $\emptyset$'s at all the nodes.

(iii) Boundary conditions _____

The assembled equations given by equation (8.7) are singular. At this stage, appropriate boundary conditions should be inserted in equation (8.7).

(iv) Solution of equations _____

The equations may be solved by one of several standard methods. In our investigations, we have used two methods. The first one is called the *tri-diagonal method of solution* and the second method is called the *frontal solution*. The attraction of the first depends on the small bandwidth of the matrix K_s, whereas the latter's attraction is strong if the main memory of the computer system is a scarce resource.

8.3 COMPUTER PROGRAM

The finite element method is readily programmed on a computer, and in fact the procedure would be of little use if computers were not available to solve the simultaneous equations that result from the descretization process.

The typical finite element program is composed of a series of common modules, which may have different uses in different contexts. Typical modules are:

(i)   Data input and display

(ii)   Element characteristics

(iii)   Assembly of equations

(iv)   Equation-solving procedures

(v)   Results and display

In programming applications, these modules appear as subroutines. It is convenient if the interfaces and data structure of these subroutines are standardized sufficiently that they may be used interchangeably.

In such systems, the master driving program is a simple routine whose only function is calling the various subroutines in appropriate order, as shown in Fig. 8.4.

In the internal operations of a finite element program, four fundamental sets of data are required. They are:

(i)   Node (vertices) coordinates

(ii)   Element labels

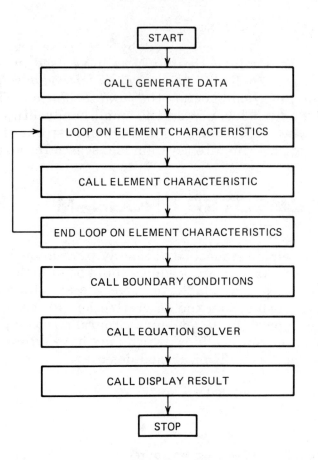

Figure 8.4 Master driving program

(iii) Physical properties of material

(iv) Boundary conditions

The output is usually a display or printout of unknown quantities which may be voltages, temperatures, velocities, and so on. One of the major practical problems of the finite element analysis is the voluminous input and output required and produced by the analyzer phase. This drawback could be removed with the use of interactive graphic support.

8.4 INTERACTIVE GRAPHIC PACKAGES TO SUPPORT THE FINITE ELEMENT ANALYSIS

One of the important parts of any finite element analysis is the input and output of data needed for the solution. In the past, this was a very tedious and time-consuming operation, as the complex element meshes, representing the idealized mathematical model corresponding to the physical phenomena being studied, had to be drawn by hand and more recently by plotting machines. The field of computer graphics, with suitable low-level software and proper hardware, offers a much more efficient way of dealing with the input and output of the data.

8.4.1 Basic Graphic Hardware

Basic graphic hardware used is a Tektronix graphic terminal with a hardcopy unit. The Tektronix was connected to a mainframe CDC Cyber 170 computer.

The hardcopy capability provided by the Tektronix unit allows the user to make a permanent reproduction of the problem descriptions and solutions. The option for hard copies is included in the program.

8.4.2 Basic Graphic Software

We are interested in using computer graphics in order to simplify the mesh generation of data needed by finite element programs. Also, it would be advantageous to display the final solution of a finite element program. In achieving these ends, software was needed so that graphics programs could be written to use the power of the CDC Cyber 170 in conjunction

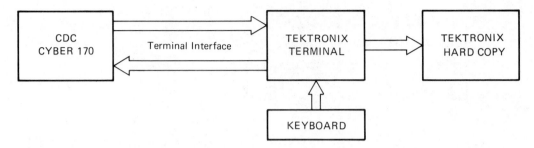

Figure 8.5 Basic hardware configuration

with the graphics capabilities of the Tektronix graphic terminal (Figs. 8.5, 8.6). The PLOT10 graphics package was used as a basic graphics software. This package provides the capability to draw points, lines, planes, characters, and so on. PLOT10 is a set of FORTRAN callable subroutines. An application program, written in FORTRAN and executed on the Cyber 170, creates display files by calling on routines in the PLOT10 package. These display files are stored in arrays until the user decides to send them to the Tektronix graphics terminal.

The software package is general purpose in nature, and can be used for a variety of applications. The software was written in FORTRAN because that is the language of most finite element programs, but other advantages were realized; in particular, the library is modular and well-structured. Also, since it is written in such a common language,

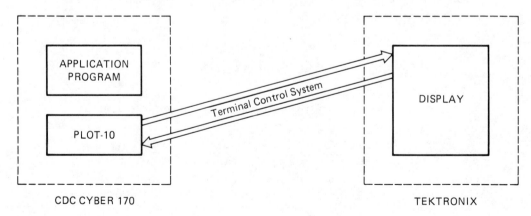

Figure 8.6 Basic software configuration

the package could be run on other machines with little difficulty.

8.4.3 High-Level Graphic Software to Generate the Required Data

The *finite element interactive graphic package* is a collection of FORTRAN routines written for use on a Tektronix graphic display terminal in conjunction with a PLOT10 basic graphic software. The package utilizes the power of the CDC Cyber 170 computer. The overall structure of the package is shown in Fig. 8.4 and the detail description is given in Fig. 8.9. Written for use with the Tektronix, these routines allow the user to develop interactively the solution of a field problem.

(i) Gross triangulation of a semi-circular domain _____

Note that only the solid line would be displayed at this stage. Curved boundaries will be considered later.

Lines joining domain points become gross triangle sides as shown in Fig. 8.7. The sides are numbered as follows: The side joining the domain points m and n will be assigned the number $((10 \times m) + n)$ if m is a one-digit number and $((100 \times m) + n)$ if m is a two-digit number, where m is the minimum of m and n. This assures that a side common to two triangles will be assigned the same number for both triangles.

This manual gross triangulation has the advantage of allowing a grading of the mesh as well as making it possible for

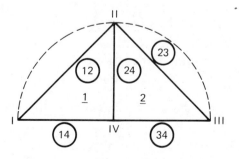

Figure 8.7 Gross triangulation of a semi-circular domain

triangle sides to be made to coincide with domain interfaces or discontinuities.

Boundary information is then entered according to gross triangle side numbers. All nodes of the meshed domain which lie on side mn will be assigned the same boundary value. Boundary values at individual nodes may be changed, entered, or removed from the list of boundary values after meshing is completed. Curved boundaries are also allowed. A user indicates which triangle sides are curved and supplies a FORTRAN function defining the curve joining the end points of each curved side. This function must be compiled and then linked with the program.

(ii) Generating a triangular mesh _____

Gross triangles are meshed one at a time in the order they were defined. Let K be the meshing factor chosen; then each triangle is meshed into K^2 elements, all similar to the gross triangle in the following manner: The gross triangle sides are divided into K sections by generating $K - 1$ nodes along each side. If the side being meshed is curved (maximum of one curved side per triangle), the nodes on the curve are found by taking the point of intersection of the perpendicular to the triangle side and the given curve at each of the $K - 1$ nodes along the side. The nodes on the curve thus generated are used along with the nodes on the other two sides to generate interior nodes at the intersection points of lines joining nodes on the curved side with the nodes on the other two sides. In Fig. 8.8, $K = 4$, nodes I, II, and III are triangle vertices and the sides are labeled 12, 23, and 13. The nodes are shown numbered in the order they are generated.

If a node has node number M, then its coordinates are found in the Mth position of the coordinates array.

The triangular elements of the mesh are defined by the node numbers of the three nodes forming its vertices. Elements are defined during the generation of interior nodes.

(iii) Meshing of sides common to two gross triangles _____

A question arises when the gross triangles have a side in common: Has the side node currently being generated been generated for a previous gross triangle? It is desirable to save the coordinates of each node only once. The most obvious way

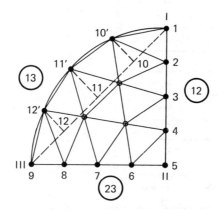

Figure 8.8 Generating a triangular mesh

to avoid duplicate storage is to search the list of node coordinates and save only new nodes. A shorter search results if
the triangle side numbers are flagged as the sides and
meshed, it then being a simple matter to determine whether
or not a particular side has been meshed. This also eliminates
any repeated calculation of node coordinates. It is not only
necessary to know whether or not a particular node already
exists, the node number must also be available for the definition of new elements. This may be accomplished by saving
the node number of the first non-vertex node of each side
along with the side number. The numbers of all other nodes
along the side may be found by incrementing the stored node
number. As the nodes of a gross triangle are generated, the
node numbers are stored in the upper left triangle of a square
array to facilitate the definition of the elements of the gross
triangle.

(iv) Node ordering _____

Nodes in the meshed domain are ordered using a reverse
Cuthill-MacKee method which yields a finite element matrix
with a near optimal bandwidth and profile, while being very
competitive from an execution time standpoint.

(v) Results and discussions _____

The meshing package as described has been tested as a subroutine of a total finite element package. (See Fig. 8.9 for a

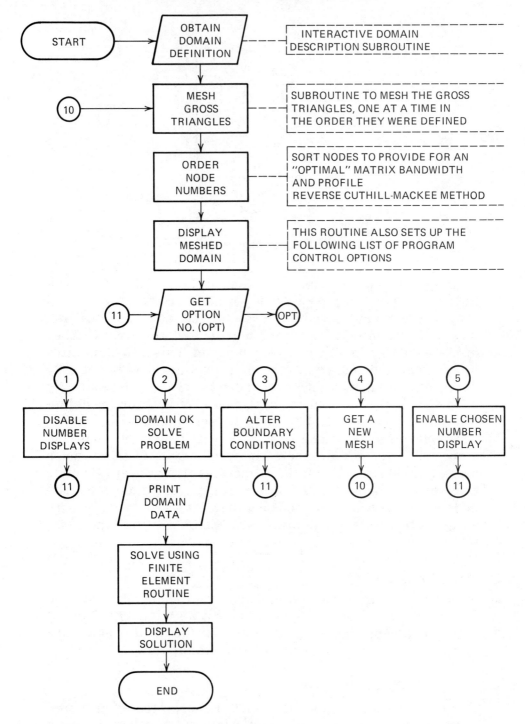

Figure 8.9 Finite element package flowchart

flowchart.) The interactive nature of the package allows rapid solutions to finite element problems, while the graphical displays simplify domain description and allow instant visual verification of the effect of each user action. The solutions of three problems are shown in the following photographs, with the first six photographs showing the major steps involved. A problem arises if a fine mesh is desired, since the displays may become cluttered and meaningless. This will not, however, affect the final results. The only other problem encountered has been the description of a curved boundary.

SUMMARY

In this chapter, an application of computer graphics to engineering science problems is described. The relationship between basic computer graphics software, computer graphics hardware, and application program is shown. The finite element method to solve field problems is briefly described. It is shown that use of computer graphics simplifies the input and output for a finite element program.

Solving the equation $\Delta^2 w \dfrac{1}{\mu}\dfrac{dp}{dz} = 0$ for the velocity distribution of viscous flow through a circular pipe.

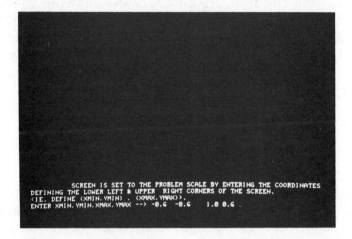

Set the scale of the screen to fit the problem in question.

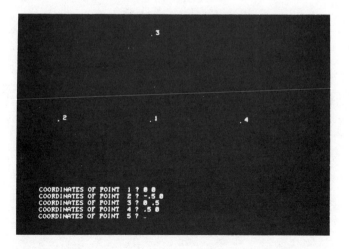

Define the domain circle center at (0,0) and diam. = 1'.

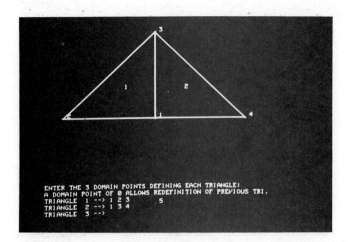

Perform the gross triangulation.

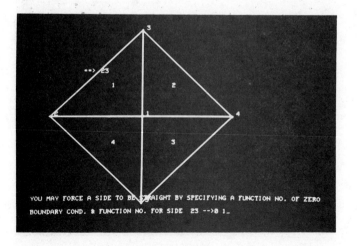

Define boundary conditions.

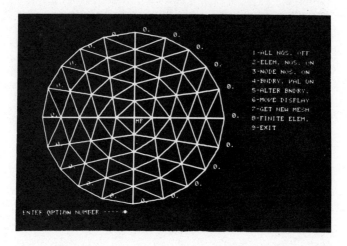

Mesh display and option list, with option
#4 shown.

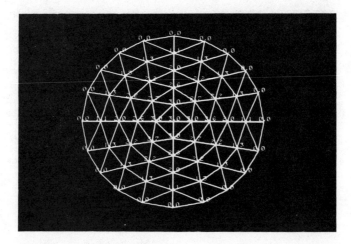

Finite element solution.

For comparison we solve the same problem for a square pipe, one foot to a side.

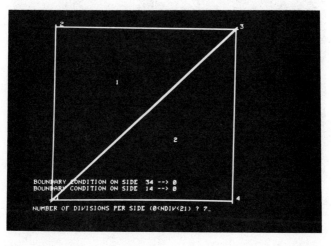

Domain description.

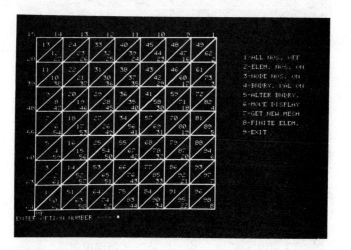

Options 2 and 3: Display node and element numbers.

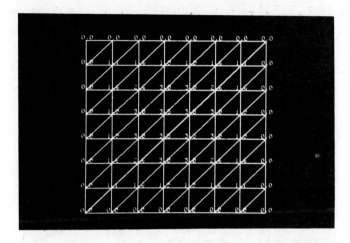

Finite element solution to velocity distribution.

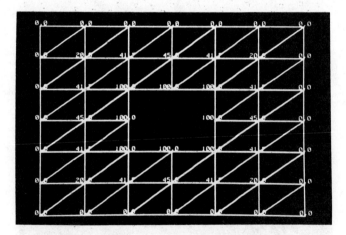

Finite element solution to Laplace's equation $\nabla^2 V = 0$ for the voltage distribution on a 150″ square plate with a 50″ square hole in the center. Boundary conditions are 100 volts at the inner edge and 0 volts at the outer edge.

REFERENCES

Agrawal, A. B., Mufti, A. A., and Jaeger, L. G., "Band Schemes vs. Frontal Routines in Non-linear Structural Analysis," *Inter. Journal Num. Methd. Eng.,* 15, 753–766, 1980.

George, John Alan, "Computer Implementation of the Finite Element Method," University Microfilms, Ann Arbor, Michigan, March, 1971, 72-5916.

Irons, B. M., "A Frontal Solution Program for Finite Element Analysis," *Inter. Journal Num. Methd. Eng.,* 2, 5–32, 1970.

Newman, W., and Sproul, R., *Principles of Interactive Graphics* (New York: McGraw-Hill Book Company, 1973).

Zienkiewicz, O. C., *The Finite Element Method in Engineering Science* (New York: McGraw-Hill Book Company, 1971).

9
COMPUTER GRAPHICS USING MICROCOMPUTERS

9.1 INTRODUCTION

With the current trends toward the increased use of micro-computers in education, business, industry, medicine, law, technology, and many other fields, including leisure at home, we should study interactive computer graphics using micro-computers.

The microcomputer is certainly an affordable computer for personal use. The advent of microcomputers is one of those milestones of technology which mark the beginning of a new and personal way to accomplish work and express crea-tivity. However, we should note that there is a classification of digital computers based mostly on complexity. The classification commonly includes microcomputers, minicomputers, medium-sized computers, large computers, and super computers (these are commonly called micros, minis, midis, main frames, and super computers).

Interactive computer graphics involves a considerable amount of dialogue between the user and the computer. The screen of a storage tube graphics terminal rapidly becomes cluttered by this dialogue, forcing the operator to erase and redo his display. Another difficulty occurs when a refresh graphics terminal is connected to a time-sharing computer system. This leads to an unreasonable demand on the computer to send the display many times per second at a high rate of data transfer. These difficulties can be avoided by having some form of local memory at the terminal. The use of microcomputers to do graphics seems to be one of the answers to reduce the load on the main computer. Further, in many applications, the power of a microcomputer may be sufficient to achieve the solution.

In order to focus on ideas and to show applications in interactive graphics using microcomputers, the following sections will present an in-depth description of one interactive computer graphic system, the Bell & Howell microcomputer system. The basic technology has its roots in the Apple microcomputers manufactured by Apple Computers, Inc.

It should be emphasized that the microcomputer category is relatively new. Microcomputers emerged at the begin-

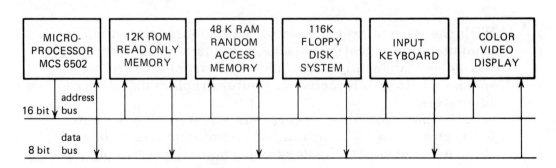

Figure 9.1 Block diagram of the Bell & Howell hardware

ning of the 1970s when improved integrated circuit (IC) technology made it possible to put a complete simple central processing unit (CPU) on a single chip. There are a variety of manufacturers and their names could be found in almost all books on microcomputers or computer organization. The interested reader will have no difficulty getting information on these popular computers from another source.

9.2 FUNCTIONAL DESCRIPTION OF THE BELL & HOWELL GRAPHIC SYSTEM

Figure 9.1 shows the architecture of the hardware. The MCS 6502 microprocessor of MOS Technology is connected through buses to the various components that support it: 48K bytes of random access memory and 12K bytes of read only memory. This memory is divided into 10K bytes of floating point BASIC and 2K bytes of system monitor; 116K-byte floppy disk system to manipulate program and data files through simple BASIC statements; ASCII standard keyboard; video display text and color graphics; and eight peripheral board connectors to expand the system with printers, tablets, and other graphic peripherals. Also available are communications capabilities to talk to other computers. Figure 9.2 shows a photograph of the Bell & Howell system.

9.2.1 Screen Format

Three different kinds of information, often referred to as "modes," can be drawn on the video display or television monitor. These modes are: text, low-resolution graphics, and high-resolution graphics.

In the text mode, 24 lines of numbers, special symbols, and upper-case letters can be drawn. Each line can have up to 40 characters. These characters are formed in a dot ma-

Figure 9.2 Bell & Howell system

trix, seven dots high and five dots wide. There is a one-dot-wide space around a character.

In the low-resolution graphics, a picture can be displayed on the screen in an array 40 blocks wide and 48 blocks high (see Fig. 9.3). In Chap. 3, these blocks were referred to as rasters, a term taken from television technology. The color of each block can be selected from a set of sixteen different colors. These colors are listed in Table 9.1. There is no space

DECIMAL	COLOR	DECIMAL	COLOR
0	Black	8	Brown
1	Magenta	9	Orange
2	Dark blue	10	Grey 2
3	Purple	11	Pink
4	Dark green	12	Light Green
5	Grey 1	13	Yellow
6	Medium blue	14	Aquamarine
7	Light blue	15	White

Table 9.1 Low-resolution graphic colors

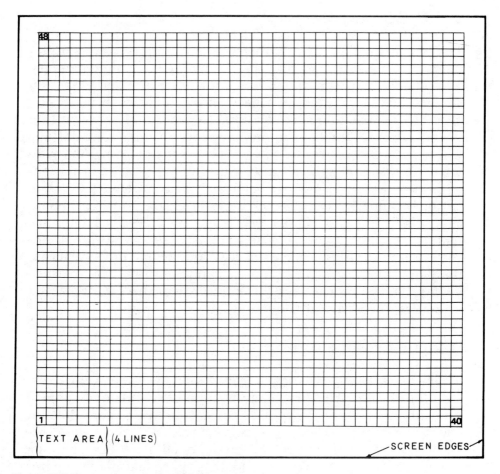

Figure 9.3 Screen format of graphics mode

between blocks, so that any two adjacent blocks of the same color look like a single, larger block. On a black-and-white television set, the colors appear as patterns of grey and white dots.

In the high-resolution graphics a picture can be displayed by color dots on a matrix 280 dots wide and 192 dots high. The dots are the same size as those which make up the text characters. There are six colors available in the high-resolution graphics mode: black, white, red, blue, green, and violet. Each dot on the screen can be either black, white, or a color.

9.2.2 Screen Memory

The video display uses information in the system's RAM memory to generate its display. The value of a single memory location controls the appearance of a certain, fixed object on the screen. This object can be a character, two stacked colored blocks, or a line of seven dots. In text and low-resolution graphics modes, an area of memory containing 1024 locations is used as the source of the screen information. Text and low-resolution graphics share this memory area. In high-resolution graphics mode, a separate, larger memory (8192 locations) is needed because of the greater amount of information which is being displayed. These memory locations are usually called "pages." The memory reserved for high-resolution graphics is sometimes called "frame buffer," as explained in Chap. 3. The name "frame buffer," or "picture buffer," indicates the fact that a picture or drawing is stored in an assigned part of the memory.

9.2.3 Screen Pages

There are actually two pages from which each mode can draw its information. The first page is called the "primary page," and the second page is called the "secondary page." Both of these pages have the same size memory allocations. The secondary page memory area follows immediately the primary page's memory area. The secondary page is useful for storing pictures or text which are to be displayed instantly. A program can use the two pages to perform animation by drawing on one page while displaying the other and flipping pages.

9.3 SOFTWARE FOR BELL & HOWELL SYSTEM

As explained before, the Bell & Howell system has 12K bytes of ROM. The 10K bytes of ROM are used for the floating-point

BASIC language and the remaining 2K bytes are used for the monitor. It should be noted that when software is built into hardware it is referred to as firmware. In other words, when we switch on the system this basic software is available to do programming. The BASIC used is an expanded version of Microsoft's floating-point BASIC. It has three data types— REAL, Integer, and String; array capability; and extensive mathematical, logical, and string functions to aid the programming. The computer graphics capabilities are built into the BASIC language. Two levels of graphics are available: low-resolution computer graphics provides 40 horizontal and 48 vertical divisions of the screen and fifteen colors, and high-resolution graphics provides 280 horizontal and 192 vertical divisions of the screen and six colors. The divisions of the screen are often referred to as pixels or rasters.

The Bell & Howell system is not restricted to only the BASIC language; it also has available PASCAL and FORTRAN languages. However, to use the latter, one requires additional random access memory of 48K bytes for each language and one disk drive. The resident monitor allows screen editing, cursor control, scrolling, and other useful commands. The addition of a floppy disk extends the capabilities of the Bell & Howell system. The floppy disk system consists of an intelligent interface card, a powerful Disk Operating System (DOS). The combination of a ROM-based monitor and an operating system in 16K-byte RAM provides the user with a comprehensive disk-handling capability.

A floppy disk gives a storage capacity of 116K bytes, which could be used to store programs and data. DOS provides for fast file retrieval. This allows one to build a program library. Command interpretation and file handling are controlled by software automatically loaded into RAM when the system is switched on.

There is a wealth of software available. The application areas are small business management and accounting, computer graphics and plotting, personal and entertainment software, and finally computer-aided learning.

9.4 PROGRAMMING

All computer graphics programming relevant to this chapter is done in BASIC language. As explained earlier, there are two graphic modes to be used. The commands for both the modes are callable from a BASIC computer graphics program.

9.4.1 Programming in Low Graphic Mode

In low-resolution graphics mode, we can use the following commands:

> GR: To use the screen in low graphic mode
> TEXT: To use the screen in the text mode
> COLOR: To choose color (see Table 9.1)
> PLOT: To put a block on the screen
> HLIN: To draw a horizontal line
> VLIN: To draw a vertical line

Suppose a light blue horizontal line is to be drawn. This could be done by the following commands:

> COLOR = 7
> HLIN 0, 39 at 20

This draws the line at the middle but across the screen.
Similarly, a light blue vertical line could be drawn by giving the following commands:

> COLOR = 7
> VLIN 0, 39 at 20

To draw a diagonal line across the screen, the command PLOT has to be used. There are two ways to do this—the first one, which is simple but will require lots of typing, is:

```
COLOR = 7
PLOT 0,0
PLOT 1,1
PLOT 2,2
      .
      .
      .
      .
      .
      .
PLOT 39,39
```

This requires 41 lines to be typed. Alternately, a simple program in BASIC will do the same thing as shown:

```
10    COLOR = 7
20    FOR I = 0 to 39
30    PLOT I,I
40    NEXT I
```

Figure 9.4 Staircase effect in the diagonal line

Figure 9.5 Vertical line

Figure 9.6 Horizontal line

There are several difficulties to be noted. These are shown in Figs. 9.4, 9.5, and 9.6.

1. The thickness of horizontal and vertical lines are such that only qualitative graphics could be done. By this it is implied that the accuracy normally required in engineering drawings cannot be achieved.

2. The staircase effect in the diagonal line cannot be avoided in raster scan graphics without further modifications to the hardware and software.

The low graphic mode could still be used to write programs to bounce balls, move lines, or erase lines to give the impression of motion. These techniques are often employed to program games. For example, to draw a diagonal line and to erase it, the above program could be modified to:

```
10   COLOR = 7
20   FOR I = 0 TO 39
30   PLOT I,I
40   NEXT I
50   COLOR = 0
60   FOR J = 0 TO 39
70   K = 39 - J
80   PLOT K,K
90   NEXT J
     .
     .
     .
```

This program will give an impression of a diagonal line being drawn from one corner of the screen to the other. On completion, it will start erasing from the final corner to the initial corner.

9.4.2 Programming in High-Resolution Graphics

In this section, high-resolution graphics will be used to draw pictures. The high-resolution graphics screen comprises

280 × 160 plotting points. The horizontal coordinates start at 0,0 at the top left corner of the screen and extend to 279,159 at the bottom right corner of the screen.

High-resolution graphics commands are similar to low-resolution graphics commands except for the addition of an H (for high resolution).

There are outputs from two programs shown in the following pages in Figs. 9.7 and 9.8. The first draws axes in x and y directions and draws a diagonal line. The second draws a house with hidden lines removed. Both these programs indicate that high-resolution graphics is much more useful and sophisticated. It is sophisticated in the sense that we can implement three-dimensional graphics on the Bell & Howell system. However, it still has some of the same difficulties found in low-resolution graphics, specifically, accuracy and the staircase effect.

Figure 9.7 Diagonal line using high-resolution graphics

Figure 9.8 House with hidden line removed

9.5 Comments on Computer Graphics Using Microcomputers

As shown in the previous sections, microcomputers can be successfully used to study elementary concepts of computer graphics, including color graphics. The elementary concepts of color were discussed in Chap. 1, and some programming which explained color graphics was shown in this chapter. However, several issues were omitted from the discussion. The important one was how to choose color for a certain part of the picture. For example, drawing a map of Canada with a different color for each province is in the domain of art. These discussions are not pursued here because these are beyond the scope of this book. However, those readers who will have access to systems such as the Bell & Howell can experiment with these ideas. Another important issue yet to be resolved is whether color graphics and the high-resolution graphics of the Bell & Howell system could be used in the area of computer-aided engineering. More work will be required to have a conclusive answer. The qualitative work in computer graphics seems to be achievable with microcomputers.

SUMMARY

In this chapter, a microcomputer system is shown to be effective in teaching elementary concepts about computer graphics. The concepts of screen pages, screen memory, low-resolution graphics, and high-resolution graphics are discussed. The BASIC programs are written to show two- and three-dimensional graphics using the Bell & Howell system.

REFERENCES

Bell & Howell Microcomputer Systems, Weston, Ontario, Canada.
  (a) Reference Manual
  (b) Floating-Point BASIC Tutorial Manual

Tomek, Ivan, *Introduction to Computer Organization* (Rockville, Maryland: Computer Science Press, 1981).

APPENDIX
ELEMENTARY
MATRIX ALGEBRA

1 MATRICES

A two-dimensional matrix is defined as a rectangular array of symbols or numerical quantities arranged in rows and columns. The array is enclosed in brackets, and thus if there are m rows and n columns, the matrix A can be represented by

$$
A = \begin{bmatrix}
a_{11} & a_{12} & a_{13} & \cdots & \cdots & a_{1n} \\
a_{21} & a_{22} & a_{23} & \cdots & \cdots & a_{2n} \\
a_{31} & a_{32} & a_{33} & \cdots & \cdots & a_{3n} \\
\cdot & \cdot & \cdot & & \cdot & \cdot \\
\cdot & \cdot & \cdot & & \cdot & \cdot \\
\cdot & \cdot & \cdot & & \cdot & \cdot \\
a_{m1} & a_{m2} & a_{m3} & & \cdot & a_{mn}
\end{bmatrix}
$$

where the typical element a_{ij} has two subscripts, of which the first denotes i^{th} row and the second denotes j^{th} column.

A matrix with m rows and n columns is defined as a matrix of dimension mxn. FORTRAN language allows specification of such a matrix by a declaration statement such as DIMENSION $A \times (20,21)$. Thus, matrix A has 20 rows and 21 columns. In this text, whenever a matrix is used in a computer program the declaration statement has been used. If $m = n$, then the matrix is called a square matrix.

2 ROW AND COLUMN VECTOR

If $m = 1$, then the matrix A reduces to a row vector with n columns

$$A = [a_{11} \quad a_{12} \quad a_{13} \quad \cdots \cdots \quad a_{1n}]$$

If $n = 1$, then the matrix A reduces to a column vector with m rows

$$A = \begin{Bmatrix} a_{11} \\ a_{21} \\ a_{31} \\ \cdot \\ \cdot \\ \cdot \\ a_{m1} \end{Bmatrix}$$

3 EQUALITY, ADDITION, AND SUBTRACTION OF MATRICES

If two matrices A and B are of the same order—i.e., have the same m and same n, then equality, addition, and subtraction are defined. To equate, add, or subtract two matrices, the operation of equality, addition, or subtraction is applied to each of the corresponding elements.

Thus, if

$$A = B$$

then

$$a_{ij} = b_{ij}$$

This implies that each element of the matrix A in a specified position is equal to the element in the corresponding position of the matrix B.

To add two matrices A and B to form a third matrix C, we perform the operation:

$$C = A + B$$

where

$$c_{ij} = a_{ij} + b_{ij}$$

This implies that each element of the matrix A in a specified position has to be added to the element in the corresponding position of the matrix B.

To subtract matrix B from A to form a third matrix D, we perform the operation:

$$D = A - B$$

where

$$d_{ij} = a_{ij} - b_{ij}$$

This implies that each element of the matrix B in a specified position has to be subtracted from the element in the corresponding position of the matrix A.

4 MATRIX MULTIPLICATION

To multiply a matrix A with a matrix B, we have to have as many columns in the matrix A as there are rows in the matrix

B. This condition is often referred to as *conformability of two matrices*.

If

$$A = \begin{bmatrix} a_{11} & a_{12} & a_{13} \\ a_{21} & a_{22} & a_{23} \end{bmatrix}$$

and

$$B = \begin{bmatrix} b_{11} & b_{12} \\ b_{21} & b_{22} \\ b_{31} & b_{32} \end{bmatrix},$$

then

$$E = AB = \begin{bmatrix} a_{11}b_{11} + a_{12}b_{21} + a_{13}b_{31} & a_{11}b_{12} + a_{12}b_{22} + a_{13}b_{32} \\ a_{21}b_{11} + a_{22}b_{21} + a_{23}b_{31} & a_{21}b_{12} + a_{22}b_{22} + a_{23}b_{32} \end{bmatrix}$$

The elements of *E* matrix are obtained by multiplying the row of matrix *A* with the appropriate columns of the matrix *B*. The general formula used in programming is to find an element e_{ij} of the matrix *E* as:

$$e_{ij} = \sum_{R=1}^{n} a_{iR} b_{Rj}$$

where

n = number of columns of *A* or number of rows of *B*

Σ = summation sign. Summation performed on the subscript R.

Thus, for $n = 3$

$$e_{ij} = a_{i1} b_{1j} + a_{i2} b_{2j} + a_{i3} b_{3j}$$

and for $i = 2, j = 1$

$$e_{21} = a_{21} b_{11} + a_{22} b_{21} + a_{23} b_{31}$$

5 DETERMINANT OF A SQUARE MATRIX

The determinant of a square matrix *A* is denoted by $|A|$. The determinant has many useful properties in matrix algebra. For our purpose, it is sufficient to illustrate the method for finding the determinant of a 3×3 square matrix.

If

$$A = \begin{bmatrix} a_{11} & a_{12} & a_{13} \\ a_{21} & a_{22} & a_{23} \\ a_{31} & a_{32} & a_{33} \end{bmatrix},$$

then

$$|A| = \begin{vmatrix} a_{11} & a_{12} & a_{13} \\ a_{21} & a_{22} & a_{23} \\ a_{31} & a_{32} & a_{33} \end{vmatrix} = a_{11} \begin{vmatrix} a_{22} & a_{23} \\ a_{32} & a_{33} \end{vmatrix} - a_{12} \begin{vmatrix} a_{21} & a_{23} \\ a_{31} & a_{33} \end{vmatrix} + a_{13} \begin{vmatrix} a_{21} & a_{22} \\ a_{31} & a_{32} \end{vmatrix}$$

Further simplification is:

$$|A| = a_{11}(a_{22}a_{33} - a_{23}a_{32}) - a_{12}(a_{21}a_{33} - a_{23}a_{31}) + a_{13}(a_{21}a_{32} - a_{22}a_{31})$$

6 INVERSE OF A SQUARE MATRIX

There are several algorithms for calculating the inverse of a square matrix. The FORTRAN language usually has a subroutine available in its library or is capable of calling a subroutine from public libraries to invert a matrix.

In matrix algebra, if we are given three simultaneous equations such as:

$$a_{11}x_1 + a_{12}x_2 + a_{13}x_3 = R_1$$
$$a_{21}x_1 + a_{22}x_2 + a_{23}x_3 = R_2$$
$$a_{31}x_1 + a_{32}x_2 + a_{33}x_3 = R_3$$

These can be written in a matrix form:

$$\begin{bmatrix} a_{11} & a_{12} & a_{13} \\ a_{21} & a_{22} & a_{23} \\ a_{31} & a_{32} & a_{33} \end{bmatrix} \begin{Bmatrix} x_1 \\ x_2 \\ x_3 \end{Bmatrix} = \begin{Bmatrix} R_1 \\ R_2 \\ R_3 \end{Bmatrix}$$

or in a concise matrix notation as:

$$Ax = R$$

The solution can be obtained by:

$$x = A^{-1}R$$

where A^{-1} is inverse of the matrix A. A matrix inverse will exist if the matrix is square and non-singular—i.e., the determinant of the matrix is other than zero.

The important property of a matrix inverse is that for any square matrix A, the equality $AA^{-1} = I$ is valid where I is an identity matrix.

To see these operations, consider the following three equations:

$$x_1 + 2x_2 + 3x_3 = 2$$
$$x_1 + 3x_2 + 3x_3 = 1$$
$$x_1 + 2x_2 + 4x_3 = 1$$

In matrix form, these equations are:

$$\begin{bmatrix} 1 & 2 & 3 \\ 1 & 3 & 3 \\ 1 & 2 & 4 \end{bmatrix} \begin{Bmatrix} x_1 \\ x_2 \\ x_3 \end{Bmatrix} = \begin{Bmatrix} 2 \\ 1 \\ 1 \end{Bmatrix}$$

In the concise matrix notation:

$$Ax = R$$

therefore,

$$x = A^{-1}R$$

or in the expanded form

$$\begin{Bmatrix} x_1 \\ x_2 \\ x_3 \end{Bmatrix} = \begin{bmatrix} 6 & -2 & -3 \\ -1 & 1 & 0 \\ -1 & 0 & 1 \end{bmatrix} \begin{Bmatrix} 2 \\ 1 \\ 1 \end{Bmatrix}$$

This gives x by multiplying A^{-1} to R

$$\begin{Bmatrix} x_1 \\ x_2 \\ x_3 \end{Bmatrix} = \begin{Bmatrix} 7 \\ -1 \\ -1 \end{Bmatrix}$$

The equality of the matrices gives

$$x_1 = 7, \ x_2 = -1, \text{ and } x_3 = -1$$

By multiplying the two matrices A and A^{-1}:

$$\begin{bmatrix} 1 & 2 & 3 \\ 1 & 3 & 3 \\ 1 & 2 & 4 \end{bmatrix} \begin{bmatrix} 6 & -2 & -3 \\ -1 & 1 & 0 \\ -1 & 0 & 1 \end{bmatrix} = \begin{bmatrix} 1 & 0 & 0 \\ 0 & 1 & 0 \\ 0 & 0 & 1 \end{bmatrix}$$

we get an identity matrix. Therefore, the matrix A^{-1} is the inverse of the first matrix A.

INDEX

D

Matrix (*Contd.*)

    of intensity, 37
    non-singular, 201
    pitch, 126
    plotters, 20
    roll, 126
    rotation, 109, 126, 127
    row, 43
    scaling, 109, 111, 127
    sparse, 137, 140
    square, 198, 200, 201
    subtraction, 198
    transportation, 4, 61, 108, 109, 110, 111, 127, 128
    translation, 109, 120, 127
    transpose, 43
    two-dimensional, 197
    vector, 20
    yaw, 126
Microcomputers, 34, 183, 184, 185, 195, 196
Microseconds, 4
Min-Max test, 141, 142
Minicomputer, 3, 4, 184
Monitor, 34

P

Parametric equation of line, 49, 50
PASCAL, 16, 17, 189
Passive graphics, 17
Perspective
    projection, 120, 129, 132, 133, 136, 148
    views, 129, 131, 137, 146
PITCH, 122, 126, 127, 128
Pixels, 33, 37, 39, 40, 41, 189
PL/1, 17
Planes, 43, 57, 69
Plotters, 16, 20, 34
Point, 4, 30, 43, 69, 103, 104, 107, 127, 141
Pointers, 84, 85, 87
Polygon test, 143
Position vector, 44
Primary colors, 9
Programming, 3, 4, 14, 15, 16
Programming languages, 14
    APL, 14, 16
    ASSEMBLER, 14
    BASIC, 16, 185, 189, 190
    FORTRAN, 14, 15, 17, 64, 72, 94, 113, 145, 170, 189, 197, 200